SPANNING SILOS

Also by David A. Aaker

Managing Brand Equity
    New York: The Free Press 1991

Building Strong Brands
    New York: The Free Press, 1996

Brand Leadership (with Erich Joachimsthaler)
    New York: The Free Press, 2000

Brand Portfolio Strategy
    New York: The Free Press, 2004

Advertising Management, 5th edition (with John G. Myers and Rajeev
    Batra) Englewood Cliffs, NJ: Prentice-Hall, 1996

Marketing Research, 9th edition (with V. Kumar and George S. Day)
    New York: John Wiley & Sons, 2007

Strategic Market Management, 8th edition
    New York: John Wiley & Sons, 2008

David A. Aaker

SPANNING SILOS

The New CMO Imperative

Harvard Business School Press

Boston, Massachusetts

No part of this publication may be reproduced, stored in or introduced into a retrieval system, or transmitted, in any form, or by any means (electronic, mechanical, photo-copying, recording, or otherwise), without the prior permission of the publisher. Requests for permission should be directed to permissions@hbsp.harvard.edu, or mailed to Permissions, Harvard Business School Publishing, 60 Harvard Way, Boston, Massachusetts 02163.

Library of Congress Cataloging-in-Publication Data

Aaker, David A.
    Spanning silos : the new CMO imperative / David A. Aaker.
      p.   cm.
    ISBN 978-1-4221-2876-3
    1. Marketing—Management. I. Title.
    HF5415.13.A22 2008
    658.8—dc22

                                                    2008016212

The paper used in this publication meets the minimum requirements of the American National Standard for Information Sciences—Permanence of Paper for Printed Library Materials, ANSI Z39.48-1992.

This book is dedicated to my seven

grandchildren, who make each day a joy—

Sami, Maile, Kailyn, Devon, Cooper,

Tea Sloane, and Landon

Contents

Preface

Spanning Silos
The New CMO Imperative

Spanning silos, is, in my view, the marketing problem of our time.

My journey into the land of silos started a decade ago when I was applying brand strategy globally. Managing brands globally was an issue in most firms, from the CEO down. Country and regional managers were entrenched and convinced that their business was different than the rest of the firm, that their autonomy was a key to success (never mind that success was for many elusive), and that coordination was cumbersome and wasteful. Yet brands and the supporting marketing strategy clearly needed to go global to gain both efficiencies and effectiveness. Markets are global and dynamic—it is a reality. So I, with Erich Joachimsthaler, initiated a study of some thirty-five firms about how to go about global brand management in the light of country silos. The results were summarized in our book *Brand Leadership*. As a result of this experience, I made plans to write a book about global marketing management.

As I continued to discuss and refine brand and marketing strategy at organizations of all sorts, I realized that country silos were not the only barrier to marketing management; there were product and functional silos as well. Further, they all shared with country silos the same issues and the same solutions. Product silo executives believed that autonomy was critical to their success, had an emotional and professional stake in being able to do their own thing, and would resist any efforts to reduce their freedom of action. Functional silos—like sales, advertising, and Internet modalities—all seemed to believe that theirs was the most effective and should receive more of the budget (independent of how they would spend it). Yet organizations that had limited access to silo-spanning brand and marketing strategies and programs (because their silos failed to communicate and coordinate) had a severe competitive disadvantage that was increasingly visible.

Organizations recognizing that their silo structure, whatever its logic and benefits, was inhibiting the development and implementation of effective and efficient branding and marketing were taking action which usually involved creating or revitalizing the office of the chief marketing officer (CMO). The job, it turns out, ranges from difficult to impossible, depending on the context. Over half of these CMOs last under two years before they give up or flame out.

In order to understand the issues and the best practice approaches to deal with silo problems I talked to executives of over forty organizations, usually someone with a CMO or comparable title. The goal was to identify the silo issues and what the organizations have done about them. What has worked? What are best-practice approaches? Insights from these interviews, coupled with the experience consulting with many dozens of clients at Prophet, relevant academic research, and the prior study on global brand management, resulted in this book.

The book should be of prime interest to CMOs and their marketing team. It should also be of interest to others in the C-suite who want to understand and support the CMO challenge. And marketing professionals throughout the silo worlds looking for ways to gain leverage, resources, and synergy from their siloed organization will also benefit from the CMO roadmap laid out in the book.

The introduction describes the CMO position and discusses a half-dozen reasons why the position is needed. The next seven chapters describe seven challenges a CMO needs to face in order to become effective, whether the road is long or short, not only to reduce the barriers they face but also to achieve the CMO's ultimate goal, which is to build strong brands and offerings and to manage great marketing programs. (See figure P-1 for the roadmap to the book and to CMO success.) The final chapter considers the first ninety days of a CMO's tenure. What needs to be done first? What should be the priorities?

Spanning silos is the new CMO imperative. Although there is no right approach that works for all there are approaches that do work. This book is a road map to success for you.

FIGURE P-1

Roadmap to the book and CMO success

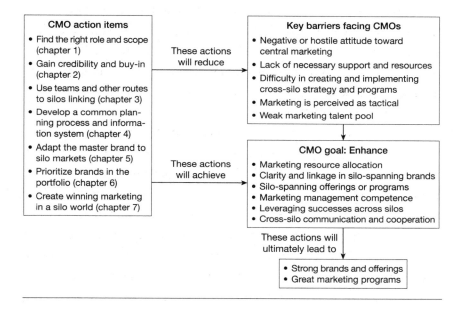

Acknowledgments

Many people helped me on this book. Erich Joachimsthaler was my colleague in the 1990s on our study of global branding, where I got a first-hand look at the country silo issue. The brand strategy team at Dentsu furthered my interest in country silos. Tom Agan worked with me on some initial interviews with CMOs around the more general silo issue and did some original thinking about the fact that all CMOs should not take on the same role. I have benefited from seeing how Prophet teams work with clients, some over a long time period, to deal with silo issues. I am in debt to all the writers and researchers who have studied global marketing management, integrated marketing communication, and the work of teams and networks. I build on the shoulders of many.

The Prophet organization has been supportive of this writing project, as it has been of others in many ways. Cindy Levine deserves a special note because of her thoughtful reviews and reactions to ideas, but many others at Prophet helped as well. Jill Steele has been a go-to person for cases and facts. Karen Woon and Amanda Nizzere supported the marketing effort.

I owe a deep debt of gratitude to CMOs and others who made time available to discuss silo problems at their organizations and what has been done and should be done about them. The willingness of these people to participate is a tribute to our field and its thrust to improve the practice of marketing management.

Thanks to Harvard Business Press and executive editor Kirsten Sandberg, who had confidence in the project and guided it along. An exceptional talent, she made numerous contributions to improve the book; she even came up with the title. Thanks also to Marcie Barnes-Henrie, who guided the book through production with unflappable ease. A special note also is due to five reviewers who provided guidance and insight. And to Charles O'Reilly and Ray Miles, two organizational behavior gurus, who helped make sure that I did not blunder as I ventured into their space. Another special thank-you goes to my daughter, Jennifer Aaker, who is a friend and colleague as well as sounding board who stimulates and encourages my endeavors. And, finally thanks to my wife, Kay, who supported yet another writing project.

The New CMO—Why?

We have met the enemy and he is us.

—Walt Kelly

In the long history of humankind (and animal kind, too) those who learned to collaborate and improvise most effectively have prevailed.

—Charles Darwin

TRUE STORY: only a few years ago, the CEO of a large global technology firm with over one hundred product business units under the same corporate brand, marketing to over a hundred countries, decided that the branding and marketing was confused, uncoordinated, and thus less efficient and effective than it could be. So he formed a central global brand unit led by the third- or fourth-ranking executive in the firm as the chief marketing officer (CMO), a person who had successfully run a major region. This executive hired a half-dozen extremely competent brand and marketing professionals. Less than three years later, all the new CMO had done was to reduce the number of corporate logos from twelve to seven. Branding and marketing remained confused, uncoordinated, and ineffective. The group disbanded and the executive left the firm. The silos won, as they so often do!

True story: a major global firm with dozens of product lines invited me to participate with a cross-silo group representing different business units and different regions. The group wanted to bring more cohesion and strategic thinking to the brand they all shared. Over several meetings, they agonized over how to convince the silo executives that (a) the lack of coordinated strategy and cohesive execution was a real problem, and (b) their combined efforts would be the solution. The group could not come up with a compelling story—and gave up. The silos won without firing a shot.

A silo is a tall, self-contained, usually sealed cylinder that often contains commodities. After a harvest, farmers use silos to store grains until they go to market. A silo is also a metaphor for organizational units that contain their own management team and talent and lack the motivation or desire to work with or even communicate with other organizational units.

From General Motors (GM) and Hewlett–Packard (HP) to Unilever and Citigroup, virtually all large organizations are collections of silos. Some, termed *product silos*, are business units defined by product or service offerings. Others, termed *country silos*, are geographic units defined by regions or countries. Still others are defined by market boundaries such as industry verticals (health care versus energy) or customer type (home consumer, business-to-business, government, *Fortune* 500, small business). There are silos within silos; for example, within product silos there may be country silos, and within country silos there may be product silos.

The quantity of product and country silos within a firm can be extensive. Firms such as Toshiba have well over one hundred business units, many of which operate in over one hundred countries—and Toshiba is not atypical. Each product or country silo or groupings of silos typically has its own marketing group charged with branding and marketing for that silo business. The existence of parallel marketing groups creates a host of problems and lost opportunities.

Although this book focuses on product and country silos, two types of functional silos share many of these issues and solutions. The first is the functional silos such as advertising, sponsorship, promotion, direct marketing, and digital marketing, some of which are outsourced. The task of creating integrated marketing communication (IMC) among them has been elusive. The different modalities instinctively regard each other as competitors rather than partners, and successful efforts to integrate their efforts are rare. When *Brandweek* asked Shelly Lazarus, CEO of Ogilvy & Mather, what she would like to go away in the new year, her reply was "silos."[1] A survey of ANA (Association of National Advertisers) members found that although 75 percent were pursuing IMC campaigns, only 25 percent rated the results as very good or better—primarily because of silo issues.[2]

The second functional silo group resides outside of marketing; examples are IT, finance, HR, service, call centers, and sales. Communication and cooperation between these functional silos, often critical to the implementation of marketing programs, can be an ongoing challenge. The frequent inability of sales and marketing to cooperate, caused in part by different perspectives and objectives, is particularly vexing.

Most organizations are rightly proud of their decentralized structure. Decentralization keeps managers close to customers and markets, on top of products and applications, ahead of competitor strategies, accountable for results, and empowered to act quickly. It also simplifies the management of complex offerings and go-to-market strategies. Strategy and tactics can be delegated to silo contexts that are relatively simple and narrow in scope. Since at least the 1920s, General Motors and other large firms have been developing and refining the principles of decentralization.

However, relying on unfettered decentralized organizations with highly autonomous silo units is no longer competitively viable. The world has changed. Markets are more dynamic with evolving boundaries. Customers are demanding silo-spanning offerings. Communication and brand building now involve multiple fast-changing modalities. Silo-spanning brands increasingly require consistency and synergies. There is a drive for marketing accountability that is inhibited by the silo structure. The need for deep expertise in cutting-edge marketing disciplines, difficult to achieve in a fragmented organization, is emerging at a rapid pace.

There is also an increasing intolerance of inefficient and ineffective marketing that is coupled with an increasing ability to discern when they are around and about. Marketing is called on to do more with less, and the inherent inefficiency of silos has become a significant burden. Resources can no longer flow to the silos with inferior return and prospects. Further, the premium on breakthrough marketing that moves the needle has never been higher, and either that never happens within silos or, if it does, the impact is muted by the silo scope.

Creating decisive competitive advantage has never been more important or elusive. Silos that operate as isolates without harnessing the insights, assets, and potential synergies of a multisilo organization lose an opportunity for advantage. When competitors do find ways to leverage a large organization, silo units can find that they are at a competitive disadvantage. Moving from silos to synergy, making the silos become part of a team, is becoming an imperative.

There is just too much at stake to allow silo interests to inhibit or prevent the effort toward achieving strong brands and effective marketing. That does not mean that the answer is to disband the silos. Some organizations can and should move toward a more centralized marketing organization while still retaining the essence of the decentralized structure. Others can and should find ways to reduce silo isolation without greatly affecting their vitality. But the process, whether slow or fast, major or minor, needs to proceed. For some firms, reducing the silo problem is the key to winning; for others, it is the key to competing; and for some, it is the key to survival.

Six Deadly Sins of a Silo Structure

Without question, changing the silo's power and function is almost always going to be arduous, expensive, and very disruptive to the organization. It takes not only financial and talent resources but investments in culture and culture change, a most precious commodity. People in silos and in the executive suite have to buy in. The cost is so high and

the task of getting cooperation from a diverse cast of characters so difficult, that the corresponding motivation needs to be visible and huge.
The *why* question is thus at the heart of the matter (see figure I-1). What
is the problem for which this is a solution? How does the CMO convince the C-suite and the silo teams that change is needed? What is the
burning platform?

The *why* question leads to the identification of at least a half-dozen
specific problems or missed opportunities that are created or worsened
by the silo structure. Individually and collectively they provide a rationale for harnessing the silo energy so that both business and marketing
strategies can emerge and succeed. It is important to understand these
problems not only to motivate change but to provide a target for change.

Marketing Resources Are Misallocated

The silo structure nearly always leads to the misallocation of resources across product and country silo units, functional teams, brands,

FIGURE I-1

Why a CMO?

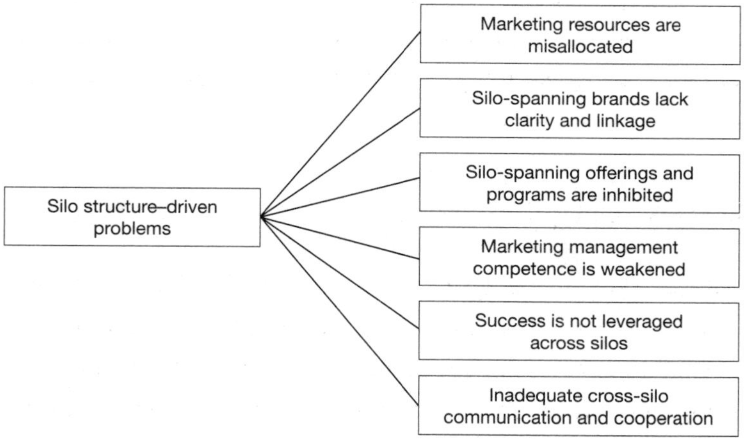

and marketing programs. Correcting misallocation, which is nearly always substantial, is the lowest hanging fruit. There is often a huge potential payoff to getting the priorities right and implementing those priorities with discipline.

Product and Country Silos. What product and country silos should receive priority? Silos' teams are organizationally and psychologically unable to make these cross-silo judgments. Nor are they equipped to do so. Such judgments require a hard-nosed analysis of the potential of the business in terms of growth, profits, and shareholder value, an analysis that compares the silos on an apples-to-apples basis. It also involves cross-silo data plus frameworks and methods that are specialized and will seldom be developed outside of a central marketing unit.

Without centrally driven discipline, allocation is usually made by political forces, with each silo telling the best story imaginable in order to retain its own cash flow and earn its share of new investments. Everyone has a growth story, even the most hopeless product and country silos. As a result, the largest and most established silos usually receive the bulk of the resources because they can pay their own way and do not appear to need painful investments of corporate resources. Yet, the large silo entities, whether they be defined by products or countries, are often mature, with limited potential for growth of sales, share, and margins. Smaller but strategically important and/or growing silos, or even product markets on the drawing board, may be superior investments of marketing resources but tend to be underfunded, to the strategic detriment of the organization.

Perhaps the worse result is that white space between silos does not get accessed at all. No silo has the perspective to see opportunities that do not fall within its boundaries, even though the organization itself may have the assets and skills to enter or even create a new category and be a winning player.

The Brand Portfolio. Increasingly, the strategic health of an organization will depend on its brand portfolio. One issue is the number of brands, especially across product silos. Without the discipline of a process managed by a central marketing group, product silos, and sometimes country silos as well, will tend to attach a new brand to new offerings. They inevitably believe that each new product is so different and so special that it merits a new brand. With the silos in charge, it is unrealistic to expect any discipline that would curb brand proliferation and foster prioritizing brands. The result is a dispersion of marketing budgets and an accompanying dilution of marketing impact.

Functional Marketing Silos. Allocating resources across functional marketing silos, such as advertising, sponsorships, PR, promotion, and digital, is from difficult to impossible. Each functional silo tends to be insular, with its own metrics and scorecard and focused on its own path to market success. Further, silo managers are not professionally dispassionate. They are interested in budget growth for reasons of personal prestige and power; plus they tend to believe in the efficacy of their own silo modality (until they are shifted to another one). Efforts to quantitatively apply marketing effectiveness models to cross-functional silo activities often find dramatic differences in the effectiveness of marketing spend. There can be, therefore, a huge payoff for making major reallocation among functional marketing silos. However, making better allocations across functional units requires data, models, experimentation expertise, and a cross-silo perspective that is usually resisted by the organization.

Marketing Programs. With silo autonomy, there is also an inability to look closely at the actual and potential returns of individual marketing programs. Even strong silos may waste marketing resources if they have weak marketing programs. Without a marketing effectiveness measurement system and a common database, organized by the central marketing group and applied across silos, the allocation is likely to go to marketing programs that will have inferior returns. The result will be not only less effective marketing at a time in which accountability pressures are intense but the starving of resources in areas of high potential and opportunity.

Silo-Spanning Brands Lack Clarity and Linkage

Too often, a master brand, perhaps even the corporate brand, is shared by many, sometimes by all, silo groups. Each silo is motivated to exploit the equity of the brand without any concern for the brand's role in other business units. They take the brand wherever the silo business dictates. There is no entity protecting the brand from being used and portrayed inconsistently. Especially when markets overlap, inconsistent product and positioning strategies can damage the brand and result in debilitating marketplace confusion. The look and feel of different brands created by disjointed colors, fonts, packaging, and presentations undercuts the synergistic potential of the firm both externally and internally.

The only way out of this nightmare is to have a central marketing group that can get control of the brand strategy. What should each of the silo-spanning brands stand for? What mechanism is there to adapt a brand to a silo context? How can brand discipline with respect to look, feel, and message be established? How are the brands linked across silos? What is common in all silo contexts? In what contexts should the use of a brand be avoided? What should the guidelines be with respect to using master brands as endorsers?

A common brand vision and strategy can motivate or even inspire the organization touched by the brand to develop marketing efforts that are "on brand." It can even affect the corporate culture by influencing the values and norms within the organization and be an impetus to the creation of synergistic brand building. Having a mixed message is debilitating to culture building as people around the world and in the different silos interact and relocate. It also makes it hard to message the organization that the brand stands for something, and it is worthwhile to have discipline in being true to that message.

When silos have control of the brand, the lack of discipline is particularly evident when new products or markets are entered. The brand is at risk when there are no guidelines or rules setting forth what products and markets will be inconsistent with the brand, and when the brand should and should not be used as an endorser. Silos need to know the conditions under which the brand is unavailable. These judgments, critical to the long-term health of the key firm assets, can best be made and enforced by a central marketing team.

Silo-Spanning Offerings and Programs Are Inhibited

An organization with many product and country silos should have a huge advantage because of the potential synergies available by creating cross-silo offerings or by developing marketing programs that multiple silos share. Sadly, when the silo barriers are in place, it becomes difficult to realize these synergies. The silo unit, by not accessing the power of the total organization, might as well be competing by itself.

Marketing Programs Shared by Silos. In today's fragmented media environment, many of the marketing program options for building brands or a customer base are infeasible, and many of the rest are not cost-effective for a silo business that lacks the necessary economies of scale. Vehicles such as sponsorships, Web sites, call centers, and even brand advertising, for example, often simply do not work effectively at a silo level because they need scale economies and coordination that can best be done centrally. In addition, resources from a central marketing team may also be more likely to have access to the best creative talent to generate a big idea and also to see it through to execution.

When silo business units are aggregated across products or countries, the economics change. Programs such as the World Cup sponsorship—the cost of which can be spread across countries and/or products—become feasible. Others simply become more efficient and effective. A hotel loyalty program like that of Starwood or Hilton becomes more efficient when it is spread over a half-dozen or more chains than when only one must cover the cost. Further, it is more effective because it enhances the value proposition for the customer. When competitors are exploiting scale economies, you are swimming upstream by clinging to a silo world.

Even cross-selling can be difficult in a silo world. Referring product customers to a service division or a banking customer to a brokerage arm or a PR customer to a sister communication company is not always easy, because there is a suspicion that the customer relationship may be damaged if the referred entity does not perform. And what is the upside for the silo executive doing the referring?

Cross-Silo Offerings. Silo barriers can seriously inhibit the development of cross-silo offerings, in part because the cross-silo collaboration needed to execute may not be in the DNA of the silos, and in part because autonomous silo units tend to look at the market with a narrow perspective and can often miss changes in the marketplace that are making their siloed offering less relevant. The result is missed opportunities and, sometimes worse, a drift toward irrelevance in the marketplace.

In many markets, the concept of having services and offerings silo based is quickly becoming obsolete. Global customers are increasingly demanding global services and offerings. They are not willing to deal with fragmented partners. Further, customers are exhibiting a preference for fewer suppliers because they want a more complete partnership and the economies and potential enhanced effectiveness that go along with it. Finally, customers can be frustrated because they are looking for systems solutions and service backup that span product silos. The movement from products to systems solutions has become a tidal wave. It was one of two major factors leading to the centralizing of marketing at Dell Services, where offerings were increasingly overlapping and even competing, and has also forced change on such firms as HP, IBM, FedEx, and many more. The CMO team can provide a role in identifying the cross-silo opportunity, creating offerings, and addressing implementation problems. At IBM, for example, the central marketing group got involved in a key barrier to silo-spanning offerings—pricing that involved internal issues as well as complex customer expectations.

The creation of a silo-spanning customer offering can give rise to a new category or subcategory. In the late 1990s, Siebel took the lead in creating Internet-based customer relationship management (CRM) by pulling together a host of application areas, including customer loyalty programs, customer acquisition, call centers, customer service, customer contact, sales force automation, and e-business.[3] Goldman Sachs repositioned its investment banking offering by combining it with its investment arm, allowing clients to have Goldman actually make debt or equity investments in its new offerings. A crucial enabler of these new go-to-market cross-silo offerings was the ability to break down the product silo barriers.

Innovations developed and paid for in one product area that can be applied in others represent a low-cost way to create new offerings and even new categories. General Electric (GE) got much of its early growth platforms by applying its early electricity generation technology to other fields, such as jet engines. Proctor & Gamble (P&G) has created advances in its detergent business from R&D in other fields, such as fragrances. Samsung cell phones draw on the flash memory business for advances, and the flash memory business has the potential to exploit those advances with other customers. A CMO can play a role in making such cross-silo opportunities become visible and come to fruition.

Marketing Management Competences Are Weakened

The quality of marketing talent, specialized support, and management sophistication tends to be dispersed and weak when silos are running their business autonomously.

Functional Capability. At one time, brand building could be delegated to an advertising agency, and focus groups plus segmentation studies were adequate marketing research. Those days are long gone. Today marketing needs to access vehicles and tools such as digital marketing, CRM programs, social networking, blog management, sponsorship management, PR in an Internet world, and on and on. Further, all of this needs more than ever to be integrated and guided by brand and marketing strategies. And marketing research is now increasingly both an art form with ethnographic research playing a large role and a science with analytical models, databases, and experimentation more central. As a result, the organization needs to be able to access specialists in a variety of areas. Further, these specialists tend to be silos of their own, so a challenge is to integrate their efforts and coordinate them as part of a bigger picture.

It simply does not make sense for a silo group to attempt to create these kinds of assets and skills; in fact, it usually is not feasible, because the silos lack scale. Further, the redundancy of having multiple marketing staff results in costly inefficiencies and limits opportunities for career advancement and specialty growth. The case for a central marketing group where such specialists can reside and be a resource for the silo groups becomes compelling. At Dell Services, another major reason that global marketing was centralized was to create a stronger, more professional marketing team that would operate without redundancy. At GE, the central marketing group aims to be a source of expertise that is respected and called on to support silo marketing teams.

Management Skills and Processes. Silos operating autonomously are often lacking in not only functional expertise but also processes and seasoned advice. Too often, silos, left on their own to develop management processes, are vulnerable to management mediocrity or worse. Rather than having an advantage of being a part of a multibusiness firm, the businesses are more likely to be at a disadvantage, competing with other firms that are capturing firmwide management capability. Management competence should not be driven by the occasional brilliant manager but should be a norm of the organization.

A CMO team can help. It can create a common marketing planning process by which all business units not only will be on the same page, but will be required to impose professional judgments about the markets, the strategic options, and the supporting programs. It can also provide guidance on both strategy and tactics and, particularly, how these can be linked to other silos, generating synergy for all.

Success Is Not Leveraged Across Silos

With a multisilo organization, pockets of brilliance may result, but they will tend to be isolated and rarely leveraged. It is not enough to have a success here and there. Maybe and occasionally is not good enough. The key to moving from good to great is to develop an organization that will identify marketing excellence whether developed centrally or within a silo and be nimble enough to leverage that excellence. To have marketing excellence only to see its application limited to a few silos, when it potentially could influence many, is tragic.

Excellence can take many forms and have many sources, but it needs to be leveraged across silos to reach its potential. It could be offerings that work. The Dockers clothing line that became a huge success for Levi Strauss, for example, originated in South America. It could be best practices involving positioning, advertising, promotion, or sponsorships. It could even be insights into customers, competitors, channels, and product technologies that could apply to many or all silos.

A firm not inhibited by silo rigidities can be more effective at rolling successful offerings and programs out to the different silo markets, particularly country-defined markets. A strong central marketing group can help manage the rollout strategy to make it more probable that first-mover opportunities will be realized. It can also enhance success probability by providing support and best-practice ideas to new introduction tactics.

Inadequate Cross-Silo Communication and Cooperation

Robust communication and cooperation, both among silos and between silos and the central marketing group, is the first line of attack against silo barriers. Communication provides access to knowledge and practice throughout the organization. Learnings of market trends, customer insights, competitor intelligence, channel dynamics, and technology developments will be enhanced if eyes and ears of all the silos can be harnessed. When cooperation is not considered or is difficult to implement, successful synergistic programs are unlikely to emerge and even less likely to be successfully implemented.

Communication and cooperation difficulties are usually created by two related factors. The first is the absence of motivation to work with other organizational groups. The silo reporting structure and performance evaluation system, both of which are tied to personal advancement and compensation, are silo defined. In most cases, there is simply no incentive to collaborate across silos or even to reach out with ideas or information. Passing on successful ideas costs silo teams precious time and effort; there is also the danger that doing so will make their counterparts' performance better and thereby reduce the relative performance of their own unit. And collaboration involves risks. There is the risk that even a worthwhile collaboration will run into execution breakdown. Even if it succeeds, there is the risk that a silo contribution will not be adequately recognized. Changing the motivation usually requires a fundamental shift in culture and values.

The second factor is the need for organizational structures and processes that will support a culture of being a team player. That means the use of teams and networks, effective information systems, focused cross-silo initiatives, interest groups that span silos, meetings that bring people together, and more. For many organizations, creating these underlying processes and infrastructure will represent a significant challenge.

Enter the CMO

Recognizing that autonomous silo organizations are no longer a viable option, a host of firms are developing, expanding, or energizing the corporate CMO position and creating or enhancing the supporting central marketing group. The role and scope of the new CMO, discussed in the next chapter, will vary, depending on the context. However, whatever the specific role and scope, the CMO will usually be charged with creating and enabling effective and efficient marketing by changing the culture, processes, structure, strategy, and people in order to reduce or eliminate silo barriers. The task is not easy, for sure.

Efforts by a CMO team to gain credibility, traction, and influence represent a formidable task in the face of silo indifference or, more likely, resistance. Succeeding and even surviving in this effort is at best uncertain. As a result, CMOs last only a few years; in one study conducted by Spencer-Stuart, the executive search firm, the tenure of CMOs was found to average twenty-three months as opposed the fifty-four months for CEOs. The amazingly short window reflects the difficulties of the new CMO's job even when the assignment is labeled to be a strategic imperative.[4]

Indicators That Decentralization Is Out of Control

- Resource allocation to product and country silos is mainly based on the prior year's budget and profitability.
- There is little accountability for marketing programs. Measures and models to evaluate programs are not available.
- Metrics and scorecards differ across silos.
- The brand portfolio suffers from overbranding and confusion.
- Silo-spanning brands do not have a consistent look, feel, and message.
- Marketing programs are not shared by silos.
- Offerings that span silos are difficult to develop and implement.
- The marketing capability is inadequate or nonexistent in key areas such as digital marketing or sponsorship.
- There is redundancy in functional marketing groups.
- The organization culture is not common across silos, nor is it strong.
- Silos do not communicate or coordinate well. There is little incentive to improve.

Reducing Silo Power: Why Is It Hard?

It does sound doable, if not straightforward. Simply reduce the silo power over strategies, budgets, and programs by centralizing and standardizing more and more activities. Why allow the silo problems to remain? It turns out that it is not simple. Firms attempting to control silo power and energy and turn silo executives into team players face several barriers. An understanding of these barriers is important when discussing the change programs needed.

CMO as a Threat. First, silo managers perceive any centralized marketing management to be a threat to them. They resist any effort to restrict their ability to control all the levers around marketing and the brand, believing that their performance, to which they are held accountable, will suffer. Removing degrees of freedom from the silos is perceived as being both unfair and unwise given that it could affect results that determine their compensation, recognition, and career path. Further, autonomy is perceived to generate energy, vitality, empowerment, local knowledge, nimbleness, and responsiveness. In contrast, centralized marketing management is, often mistakenly, viewed as necessarily moving the organization to one that would be bureaucratic, inefficient, confining, and controlling.

Resisting this perceived threat, silo managers are likely to express opinions such as the following:

"I know this arena and you do not."

"My market is different, and what works elsewhere will not work here."

"I cannot compete if I am to wait for a bureaucracy to function."

"Thank you for your suggestion, but I'll do it my way."

Such attitudes tend to be stronger when the silo marketing team has been in place for long periods. Several firms rotate key members of the silo team every two or three years to reduce the insular atmosphere. Another factor is that country silos that have unique cultures and are geographically separate tend to be more parochial. Opinions of country silo managers are in such cases more likely to have validity and be more difficult to refute.

The following is all too common. A new CMO created a global strategy involving a more upscale brand vision, a revised distribution channel, a new common logo and set of rules on visual presentation of the brands, a centralized sponsorship program, and common advertising.

There was a significant effort to change the silo organizational structure, reward system, and culture that had been making a mess of the brand portfolio. All seemed to be on track. However, in the country silos, the change was not evident, because resistant managers found ways to retain their old autonomy. The problem for which global marketing management was a solution was never understood and accepted by the silo management team. Turning global plans into global reality is difficult.

Inadequate Resources and Authority. A second barrier is a failure to provide the resources, authority, and top management resolve to make the CMO integration task successful. Many companies do decide to get serious about building brands and marketing, or so they say. They typically form brand or marketing management entities after realizing the need to create and enhance brand assets to support present and future business strategy. Often these are staffed with junior people, but sometimes with very senior executives. For a time these entities create programs and processes, or at least identify the need for them, but ultimately nothing happens and frustration sets in. The entities simply do not receive the needed authority and resources to succeed. Lip service is given in support but the tools to actually do the job are withheld or withdrawn when financial pressures appear. Ultimately, the CEO has other priorities and is not willing to support a group that, by necessity, has to be organizationally disruptive. Support is often needed as well from other top executives, such as the heads of the silo units. A great relationship with a silo marketing group could be undercut by the silo head if he or she is not on board.

Silo-Spanning Marketing Management Is Challenging. The third barrier is that the task of silo-spanning marketing management is difficult even without organizational issues. Developing marketing that has a silo-spanning scope is challenging because conceptualizing, prioritizing, and implementing marketing strategies and tactics in a multisilo organization involves complexities that are formidable. Brand strategy, for example, is hard enough without the complication that it has to work in a set of diverse product-markets.

Marketing Is Perceived as Tactical. The fourth barrier is the lack of a strategic marketing culture, which means that the problems, even those that are severe, tend not to rise to the top. Marketing has been considered tactical, something to be delegated to advertising and promotions professionals who are charged with creating short-term sales bumps. Key executives do not understand the value of a cohesive, synergistic overall brand strategy. In fact, brands are not considered as long-term assets enabling the business strategy. Even when an awakening occurs and it is realized that marketing and branding is strategic, there is enormous inertia to overcome.

Marketing Talent Is Lacking. The final barrier is the lack of marketing talent. The people to lead and staff a centralized marketing group are just not there. There may be people skilled in tactical marketing tasks. However, what is needed are people with a breadth of knowledge of the functional marketing areas, including digital marketing, and with a strategic perspective. These people are usually in short supply or not available.

From Silos to Synergy

How can silo barriers to the creation of great marketing and marketing organizations be reduced or eliminated? How can silo power be converted from an inhibitor to an enabler of effective and efficient marketing? As the book will make clear, a host of tools and options are available and used. How they are applied will very much depend on the context.

However, whatever the situation, the end goal driving change should be twofold:

- To advance the likelihood of great marketing, marketing that will impact the business and generate a high return on investment, marketing that is effective and efficient

- To develop stronger offerings and brands

In addition to these end objectives, the CMO and the central team should address the silo barriers to change and focus on six goals corresponding to the six silo structure–driven problems and missed opportunities. Advancing the cause on any one of them can affect the impact of marketing in the marketplace. The CMO should create change in the organization such that it encourages more and better:

- *Allocation of marketing resources.* Improve the allocation of marketing resources across products, countries, functions, brands, and marketing programs. Avoid the liability of putting money into low-potential or poorly performing silos or programs. Recognize that it is increasingly important to use accountability and measurement to drive the search for effective and efficient marketing.

- *Clarity and linkage in silo-spanning brand strategy.* Develop processes and organizational units that will ensure that silo units have clear and effective brand strategies that are linked to other silo units and to the brand strategy of the organization. Brand strategies drive programs. They need to be good and they need to be connected.

- *Silo-spanning marketing offerings and programs.* Create an organization in which silo-spanning offerings and programs that respond to market trends can flourish. And find ways to identify and pursue opportunities for scale (exploiting size) and scope (exploiting product, country, and functional scope of operations) economies that are real and worthwhile. Scale and scope economies are the sure routes to high return.

- *Marketing management competence.* Find ways to improve the talent and process that will make the marketing management more professional and effective. Make sure that there is coverage and critical mass in key functional areas, product units, and geographies.

- *Leveraging success.* The organization needs to foster idea sources that will generate great marketing strategies and programs and be nimble enough to identify and leverage them over silos quickly and effectively.

- *Communication and cooperation.* Create devices processes, events, organizational structures, and an information system that will enable communication and cooperation and foster a culture that allows them to flourish.

This set of objectives differs sharply from the conventional wisdom. Too often the charge or goal of the CMO is focused on what or how to change rather than the objective of fostering better brands and marketing by addressing the silo-driven problems. The objective often is to maximize centralization, bringing much of marketing under the control of the CMO, and to standardize—one offering, one position, one theme, one look, and one package. Or the objective is simply to sharply reduce the power, vitality, and competence of the silo unit or even to simply reduce the number of silos. One brief for a new CMO of a major firm was to reduce the number of agencies from twenty-six to one, as if that would immediately eliminate silo barriers to synergistic marketing. Such simplistic goals often result in dysfunctional decisions rather than improved performance.

Directionally, reducing silo authority, making the organization more centralized, and making the offering and marketing more standardized are often warranted and useful. In fact, there is a strong trend in that direction for good reason. However, these changes should not be goals in themselves but, rather, one of the routes to the set of six goals. Progress among these goals will lead to stronger offerings and brands and effective synergistic marketing strategies and programs. The result can be an organization that retains much of the decentralized structure that has served it well but with silo units that work as team members. The era of isolated islands unto themselves should end.

Creating a Road Map for CMO Success

This book is intended to create a road map for success for the CMO office that is struggling with silo-driven barriers to great offerings and marketing. Figure I-2 summarizes the thrust and flow of the book. In addition to the CMO team the book is directed at those in decentralized

FIGURE I-2

Roadmap to the book and CMO success

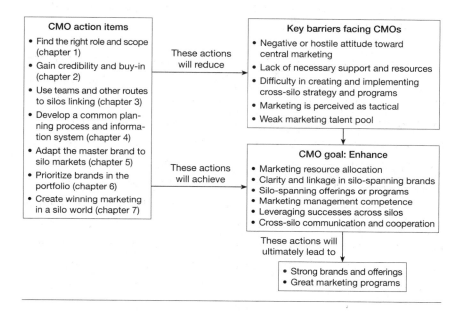

business units who are attempting to tap into the larger organization in order to make their offerings more competitive.

The book draws heavily on four sources of information to identify best practice approaches to silo issues. One was my prior work on branding, particularly on brand portfolio strategy. A second was firsthand experience with clients of Prophet, who embarked on and, in some cases, went through a process of modifying organizational structure and strategy to create synergy in the face of strong silo forces, a process that usually took many years. A third, with contributions from Erich Joachimsthaler and Dentsu Brand Consulting Group, involved discussion with top executives of some thirty-five firms about how they make global brand management successful. Firms included in these studies were selected to represent a mix of firms from service, high tech, business-to-business (B2B), durables, and packaged goods and represented Europe, the United States, Korea, and Japan.

The fourth and major source was a study consisting of interviews with executives from over forty firms. Most were CMOs or people in comparable positions and the others had visibility into the CMO office. Basically, they were asked to identify silo issues and how they handled them— what worked and what did not. The firms were selected to represent a range of industries and home countries. The set of firms included 3M, Adobe, Allstate, Barclays, BBVA (Spain), Bernesse (Japan), BP, Canon, Carlson, Caterpillar, CDW, ChevronTexaco, CIGNA, Clorox, DDB, Dell, Dentsu, Dolby, Dow Corning, Dreyer's, Fidelity, GE, GM, Google, Hitachi, HSBC, IBM, Intel, Logitech, McDonald's, Monsanto, Nestlé, P&G, Prophet, SABMiller, Seagram, Siebel, Syrutra (China), Toyota (China), UBS, Visa, and Y&R.[5]

The goal of the interviews in the last study was to determine what executives in a representative sample of firms felt were their own best practices. It was based on judgments of the executives themselves, who often had firsthand knowledge. In most cases but not all, there is no quantitative evidence that the programs noted actually had a measurable return on investment. The financial performance of firms and of silo units is due to a host of factors, many of which are exogenous to the firm. As a result, the impact of any one of them is usually impossible to measure. The existence of any type of experimental setting is either not feasible or not considered worthwhile by firms attempting to respond quickly to a dynamic marketplace and emerging challenges. Further, even if a correlation with performance can be isolated, the direction-of-causation issue can confound.

There were occasionally cases in which the vitalization of the CMO and central marketing team was widely considered a driver of a turnaround. The cases of IBM in the early 1990s and of McDonald's and BBVA (described in chapter 1) about ten years later are examples. In each case, the firm was in a crisis mode, and a strong change-agent CMO was brought in from the outside to create a brand-driven coordinated marketing program.

It is clear, given this cumulative experience pool, that the nature of the CMO task will highly depend on the market context and the organizational realities. However, there are commonalities. Any CMO needs to address in one way or another seven challenges that are discussed in the upcoming chapters. Progress in these challenges should reduce the barriers to silo cooperation and achieve progress in the six CMO goals linked to the six silo structure–driven problems.

Chapter 1—Find the right role and scope. A CMO can take on a variety of roles, from that of a facilitator to others that are more ambitious. The selection of the right role, which will vary over activities and over time, can be critical to CMO success or even survival. The determination of the country, product, and functional scope of the CMO team will balance focus and scale.

Chapter 2—Gain credibility and buy-in. A CMO needs to gain credibility and involvement in order to be heard and to influence. To that end, a CMO should attempt to gain the support of the CEO, acquire customer knowledge, show visible successes, respect and engage the silos, and upgrade the marketing staff.

Chapter 3—Use teams and other routes to silo linking. Teams are powerful ways to overcome silo issues and to change the culture. Among the other routes to silo linking are formal and informal networks, liaison roles, integrator roles, centers of excellence, matrix organizations, and centralized marketing.

Chapter 4—Develop a common planning process and information system. Creating a common planning process and information system can encourage professionalism and the exchange of information, thus influencing strategies and programs.

Chapter 5—Adapt the master brand to silo markets. There are contexts in which a brand and marketing strategy should not be standardized across silo markets because a standardized brand will not support the associations needed for a winning offering. Methods to adapt the brand to silo marketing while maintaining brand consistency are needed.

Chapter 6—Prioritize brands in the portfolio. Disciplined methods should be developed to make decisions about when to add a brand to the portfolio and when to consider the use of subbrands and endorsed brands. The key strategic master brands should be identified, prioritized, and leveraged, and the rest of the brands in the portfolio should be assigned roles.

Chapter 7—Develop winning silo-spanning marketing. Brilliant marketing programs can originate in the silos or in central marketing. The challenge is to recognize and exploit brilliance when it emerges and to decide what scope and authority the silo teams should have in implementation. Other issues include deciding on the number of communication partners, how to allocate marketing resources across silos, and how to communicate the brand and marketing program internally.

In the balance of the book, the focus will be on understanding the issues involved in a multisilo organization, the best practice tools available to deal with these issues, and the keys to success. The final chapter will suggest what the CMO should do in the first ninety days after assuming the task of leading a new or revitalized CMO office—namely, to assess where the organization is with respect to silo issues and plan the steps to take to address them.

For Discussion

1. Review the six silo structure–driven problems. Rate your organization on the severity of each of these problems using a 1-to-10 scale, where over 5 means there is a significant deficiency and under 5 indicates good performance along that problem dimension.

2. Evaluate your firm on the five barriers to reducing silo power.

3. Comment on the CMO goals set forth.

Chapter 1

Find the Right Role and Scope—The CMO's New Job Description

There is a fine line between fishing and just standing on the shore like an idiot.

—Steven Wright, comedian

There is no worse mistake in public leadership than to hold out false hopes soon to be swept away.

—Winston S. Churchill

A COMMON SCENARIO: a CEO decides that the organization needs an empowered CMO with a competent supporting staff to reign in the silo groups. Perhaps a major brand, crucial to future strategy, is being taken in different directions and is at risk. Or perhaps the marketing effort is fragmented with returns on investment that are frustratingly unknown but suspected of being dismal. Whatever the reason, the CMO comes on board and aggressively attempts to make marketing more strategic and synergetic by creating an advertising campaign with a new centralized agency or redoing the brand vision complete with new logos and brand books.

The result is a failure to achieve any of the objectives or even a dramatic flameout. In either case, the CMO quickly leaves, joining that half of CMO population with a tenure well under two years. The silos have successfully repelled an attack on their autonomy and are now free and clear for some time to come. The silos won because the necessary ingredients for CMO success were missing and the CMO attempted to do too much too fast. The Spencer Stuart study introduced in the previous chapter identified the most common cause for the short tenure of CMOs, namely unrealistic expectations in part generated by CMOs that over-promise.[1] With a less ambitious role, the outcome might have taken longer but would have been very different.

One insight is that the CMO and the central marketing group can assume a spectrum of roles. Some, such as being a facilitator, are modest and may require patience to get results. Others, taking control of an advertising program and budget, for example, have the potential for a substantial and relatively quick impact but have a higher risk profile. Of course, some contexts require an aggressive role. Being too cautious can risk failure to meet the needs and expectations of the organization. It is important to recognize where the organization is and how receptive it is to change. Is it in crisis mode with a CEO pushing for critically needed change, for example, or has it got strong established silos that appear to be working well?

Another insight is that modest roles can have a major impact on strategy, programs, and even on the culture of the organization. Affecting the decision process and information and reward systems can influence options and decisions both directly and indirectly. It is not necessary to be in control of budgets and programs in order to effect change and results.

A major complication is that the roles of the CMO can and often will vary with the activity and the silo, and additionally, will evolve over time. The CMO role for coordinating the visual presentation of a brand might involve more control and authority than that of creating a brand strategy over the silos. The nature of involvement of the CMO team with a silo business unit doing well might be very different than another that is struggling. And the roles will change over time, dictated by the credibility of the central marketing group, the motivations of the silo businesses, and by market conditions. Nothing is simple about the CMO charge.

In addition to roles, scope is another important dimension of the charge of the CMO and the central marketing group. What activities should be within the purview of the CMO—brand strategy, Internet strategy, advertising? And what silos? Which product or country silos should be combined to be influenced or managed by the CMO? Too broad a scope and the effort might lose focus and fail to deliver competence. Too narrow, and the charge to integrate and find growth opportunities will not be met.

The activity and product/country scope decision will be discussed, but I first turn to the alternative CMO roles.

Five Potential Hats: Facilitator, Consultant, Service Provider, Strategic Partner, Strategic Captain

The CMO team can assume one or more of several prototypical management roles—facilitator, consultant, service provider, strategic partner, and strategic captain—that reflect differing levels of influence and authority (see figure 1-1).

Facilitator

The *facilitator role*, the least threatening to a decentralized organization, enables business units to develop marketing strategies without the CMO team's active participation and involves tasks such as:

- Establishing a common planning framework that provides vocabulary and discipline to the planning process

- Encouraging and enabling the business units to collaborate through teams and other organizational structure devices

- Fostering communication through such devices as networks, meetings, events, and Intranet sites

- Creating data and knowledge hubs, some based on original marketing research, that all silos can use

FIGURE 1-1

Alternative CMO roles

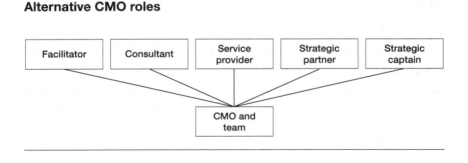

• Upgrading the level of marketing, brand sophistication, and
performance measurement

None of these tasks involve the CMO team in the strategy development and implementation of the silo businesses. The silo marketing groups
remain largely unconstrained.

The facilitator, an alternative to prematurely attempting to control the
silos that will resent an "outsider," can stimulate change that is likely to
be tolerated. The influence that a carefully conceived and implemented
facilitator role—with the CEO's support—can have on silo decisions and
performance can be surprising. Setting up formal and informal cross-
silo communication channels and establishing a common planning framework and knowledge base can encourage synergy to emerge. When silo
representatives start exchanging experiences, joint programs and other
coordinated efforts will ensue. In addition, a successful facilitator role
can lead to building credibility and relationships that will be the key to
the establishment of more influential roles. Sometimes this growth in influence can occur rapidly, but in some organizations it can take five, ten,
or more years for enablers of change to move into place. Organizations
with strong cultures, structures, and processes do not change easily.

A facilitator can reduce the risk of an early flameout. The CMO who
assumes the management responsibility of important brand-building programs such as advertising, sponsorships, and digital strategies must perform

with little margin of error—only home runs will do. The silos will exploit the first sign of a misstep to reinforce their authority and autonomy.

The next three chapters contain material designed to make the facilitator role more effective and become a platform to extend the role of the CMO team. The material includes discussions on how to gain credibility; how to use teams, formal networks, and other silo-linking devices; and the power of common planning models and information systems.

Consultant

In the CMO's second potential role, as *consultant*, the CMO team advises the silos in developing and executing marketing strategy by:

- Participating in, if not leading, the analysis of each silo business's markets, competitors, and customers

- Contributing to the generation of companywide insights

- Suggesting strategic options and marketing programs to the silo marketing groups

- Refining those options and responsive programs

The CMO's team would thus become an active—but invited—partner with the silo marketing teams.

The CMO team would add value from at least two perspectives. First, they would bring to the table expertise and experience in functional areas of marketing such as brand strategy, advertising, Internet marketing, and sponsorships. Second, they would bring a cross-silo perspective from being involved in multiple silos and from having a cross-silo perspective in their information gathering and research.

While the CMO team can recommend and even initiate brand strategy options, control remains in silo business units. The team's efforts to affect brand strategy depend on its insights and suggestions. It is an influence rather than a control model.

With a consultant model, the credibility, competence, and track record of the CMO team become critical. The CMO at 3M was one of many who indicated that the consultants need to be so respected that the silo units will ask, even demand, their participation in the relevant silo work sessions. First, impressions matter. If the initial contact of the consultants from the CMO team does not impress the silo executives, the experience is likely to revitalize a "go it alone" or even antagonistic attitude. Further, a bad experience will affect the inclinations of other silos to seek consulting help as will a positive one of course. The role of consultant can build on the facilitator role. 3M viewed its CMO team as primarily filling the facilitator and consulting roles.

Service Provider

The third potential role, *service provider*, involves the silo business units' "hiring" the CMO's team to provide such marketing services as consumer research, segmentation studies, employee training, managing sponsorships or promotions, and selecting and managing third-party suppliers. For some firms such as Clorox, with dozens of major brands, the CMO team considered the service provider role to be its dominant role in the firm.

As a service provider, the CMO team gets involved indirectly in developing marketing strategy and creating marketing programs. By conducting segmentation studies for a silo, for example, the CMO's group can guide that silo in interpreting the results and developing the segmentation strategy crucial to marketing execution and can share findings across business units, thereby fueling joint participation in program development.

A service provider role can influence and even implement strategy. The central marketing group at Carlson Hotels Worldwide (running five brands, including Radisson and Regent), trains employees on how to interact with customers, a key element to its business and brand strategy. They also provide examples of visual presentation of the brand and advertisements for the several silos to use. The silos, in this case, the hotels' autonomous franchisees have an economic incentive to use what has been developed rather than pay for an outside alternative.

Owning the relationship with the communication suppliers, especially advertising agencies, yields influence. A practical and symbolic locus of control changes when a single agency replaces multiple agencies, each owned by a silo or a group of silos. Many firms including IBM, Samsung, and Dell have consolidated agencies. As a result, a key organizational support for silo autonomy, control of its own agency, disappears.

One potential problem with the service provider role is that too often, silos tend to use the CMO teams for tactical programs and neglect to get support for strategic issues. As a result, strategic decisions are treated superficially or even ignored. Silos at Logitech, for example, looked to central marketing for testing products and programs rather than for performing research on customers and market behavior that could have led to strategic options.

The CMO team needs to exhibit a high level of competence within their service arenas and making that competence credible and visible. That means talented people, success stories, the creation of centers of excellence around functional areas like Internet marketing and sponsorships, all of which will be described in the next few chapters. Like the consultant role, the service provider role should aim to be considered a valued contributor to the silo team. BP, for example, created a segmentation strategy for one silo on the basis of quantitative research that was so successful that it was a key part of its go-to-market strategies. The other silos, observing the results, were waiting in line to have the same service. Success breeds credibility.

The risk of the facilitator, consultant, and service provide roles is that they do not necessarily create change as forcefully and as fast as is needed. The silo groups can successfully resist their initiatives and see their efforts as nothing more than another variant of "business as usual." The result can be the perception and reality of little impact. Thus, in some cases it is necessary to turn to more active roles such as that of a strategic partner.

Strategic Partner

In the fourth potential role, *strategic partner*, the CMO will always have a seat—invited or not—at the silo strategy table. The responsibility of creating and applying a marketing and branding strategy is jointly assigned. That means a team approach with collaboration. Usually, both the CMO and the silo must agree on the strategy, approve the measure of its success, engage in its implementation, and review it over time.

The locus of power and responsibility for generating strategies and implementing them might tip to one side or the other. At one extreme, the CMO may simply have approval rights and become more an adviser than a participant. With approval rights, the CMO team could make sure that the silos aligned their marketing programs with the strategy, compromised no brands, exploited potential synergies, and allocated resources according to the firmwide strategy. For many firms, the CMO team has approval authority over at least some aspects of advertising created by silos—it can make sure, for example, that the look and feel as well as the message fits the global brand strategy. Conversely, the silo team could have veto power over a CMO-driven marketing program. For example, the CMO team could put forward a set of programs including some advertisements and programs surrounding a global sponsorship, and the silo marketing groups would be free to use, adapt, or not use them.

The competence level and the underlying silo market knowledge of the CMO teams needs to be even at a higher level in the strategic partnership role than in the consultant or service provider role. And the collaboration chemistry also needs to be high. It will not work when confrontation replaces collaboration.

Strategic Captain

In the fifth potential role, *strategic captain*, the CMO team conceives, selects, and manages the marketing strategy and programs. It interprets trends and provides insights into customer and competitor dynamics. With information about new product flow and corporate strategy, the CMO team develops marketing and branding strategies and even marketing programs for silo markets. With credible brand and marketing knowledge, authority, and resources, they would actively manage the silo marketing managers whose primary job would be to adapt and implement.

The strategic captain model succeeds only when the CMO team has the highest level of competence and credibility and when the company's

CEO places a priority on marketing synergy and branding consistency, provides the CMO with resources, and visibly backs the CMO's authority.

One determinant of authority over silos is the control over the marketing budget. How much of the marketing budget falls under the CMO's charge? What elements, if any, of the budget will be under the auspices of the silo teams? In the strategic partner role, the CMO may have a significant central marketing budget and recommend budget allocation across silos. However, as a strategic captain, the CMO is likely to have greater influence if not control of the bulk of the marketing budget, its allocation, and its use. At health insurer CIGNA, only 15 percent of the marketing budget is controlled by the silos. Authority becomes somewhat irrelevant without resources.

Another key determinant of authority is the reporting arrangement. The CMO, as a strategic captain, nearly always reports to the CEO or perhaps the chief operating officer (COO). However, as a facilitator or a service provider, the CMO often reports to the chief financial officer (CFO) or the head of human resources. When seasoned CMOs were hired as change agents at both Visa and Allstate, a condition was that the post reported to the CEO and was a part of the executive team.

The CMO must play the strategic captain with sensitivity even when sufficient authority, talent, and resources are in place. Toward that end, the CMO team should listen to and work with the silo teams and explain the rationale behind the marketing and branding strategy. The CMO can even position the "logo cop" function, often viewed as bureaucratic and negative, as valuable in providing early-stage advice and communicating clear guidelines. When the logo cop function became too negative at Honda, it was transferred to the intellectual property group so that the CMO team could have a more positive relationship with the silo units.

Clearly, these five roles are not necessarily mutually exclusive. In most cases, they are cumulative. So service providers also facilitate and consult. And those classified as strategic captains will very likely take on many of the other roles as well.

Which Roles Are Right for You?

Which should be the dominate role or roles that your CMO team should play? When is the strategic captain role advisable or even feasible? When should there be a change moving up toward a strategic partner or strategic captain role? When should that change be abrupt rather than gradual? The answers depend on organizational factors such as:

- *CEO commitment.* Does the CEO visibly support synergies across silos? Does that support go beyond lip service? Will that support include participation in culture change? Will the CEO provide resources needed?

- *Marketing talent.* Does the firm have top talent within the CMO team and throughout the silos' marketing groups? Without quality marketing in the silos, the task of justifying and implementing marketing programs becomes more difficult.

- *A clear business vision.* Does the firm have a clear business vision with a supporting brand strategy that provides a compelling reason why silo units should relinquish authority? Dell's business imperative to provide systems solutions to customers rather than ad hoc products was one compelling reason for Dell Services to centralize its marketing.

- *A sense of crisis.* Nothing motivates better than dissatisfaction with present performance and trajectory. Change is hard when things seem to be going well. In 2002, McDonald's was ready for Larry Light, hired as CMO from outside to change marketing, because McDonald's financial performance was approaching the crisis point. Sometimes the CEO needs to create a sense of crisis based on future threats or growth expectations in order to stimulate change.

- *Having a CMO change agent.* Having a CMO who is a change agent with organizational clout, who is willing to take a fresh perspective and force change options on the firm, is a necessary condition to moving to a more aggressive role. Such a person is often, but not always, an outsider to the firm with credibility in marketing, a person who is not tied to the traditions and norms of the firm. Firms such as McDonald's, IBM, Allstate, Visa, Samsung, and Dell Services all had outsider change agents.

When even one of these factors is unfavorable, it can be hard to start or move up the influence chain toward a strategic captain or strategic partner role. A favorable score on one factor will not compensate for an unfavorable one on another. They must be aligned. If not, the better part of valor is to adopt the facilitator role and perhaps the consultant and service provider roles and work to remove the limiting factor or factors. Some firms will maintain these less ambitious roles as the dominant management role indefinitely because the organizational realities inhibit any other role. Not every firm should aspire to have strategic captains in the CMO office.

Two summary dimensions should help the CMO select the proper role. First is the potential payoff of creating a more aggressive role. How much will coordination and synergy help the marketing strategy? How limiting and inefficient is the present operating model? Second, how painful and expensive will changing the organization be to reduce that power? The more powerful the silos, the harder the task.

How Roles Evolve

The CMO roles can, and often should, evolve over time. Most CMO teams will value transitioning toward the strategic captain role. But how to get there and how fast? It can take many years if the organization has little traditional brand management and is highly decentralized.

Procter & Gamble (P&G) illustrates an evolution toward more centralized control that spanned decades. It moved from brand managers to category managers in the 1980s, thereby removing the product silo barriers within categories such as hair care, including brands such as Pantene, Herbal Essence, Aussie, Infusion, and Head & Shoulders. The category manager controlled the brands in the category and, for example, allocated product innovation and market spend. During the 1990s, P&G developed a regional management structure where each of eleven product categories were run by a global category team consisting of the four regional category managers with line responsibility for marketing plus R&D and manufacturing for the category within their region. An executive vice president with a "second" line job chaired the global category team. The team, responsible for the brand identity, brand position, and product innovation for brands in the category throughout the world, met five or six times a year and enhanced global coordination and synergy. In the 2000's, motivated by a need to implement global decisions faster, P&G elevated the authority and responsibility of the global category manager. There was still a global team but the executive in charge had the authority to make and implement decisions.

Although a gradual evolutionary change in the authority and control of the CMO team is common and prudent, sometimes a CEO-sponsored strategy needs a stronger CMO and brand strategy immediately to succeed, and, as a result, a significant organizational change becomes both necessary and feasible. Although disruptive, it can potentially spare the organization a lengthy transition period.

Creating an abrupt change from a silo-dominated organization to one in which the silos no longer are the focus of power does not happen often. Observing several case studies supports the hypothesis that such a change requires a strong, motivated CEO stimulated by a new business strategy, a change agent CMO with credibility, a precipitating organizational crisis, and the organizational competence needed to implement the change both internally and externally. It still takes years to implement. Two case studies illustrate.

In early 1993 Lou Gerstner took over a financially troubled IBM poised to break itself up into seven companies.[2] Gerstner decided during his first months that IBM needed to stay together and redirect itself to providing integrated solutions to customers, something that because of IBM's product breadth, technology, and systems support it was uniquely capable of doing. To achieve that objective, he had to integrate IBM itself and refocus and reenergize the brand.

Gerstner faced twenty-four product fiefdoms plus geographic silos organized around regional groupings of some 160 countries and areas within the United States. These units had the budgets and power, and focused on developing and promoting products rather than customer needs. A financial services client in Atlanta would have no access to the IBM banking experts in New York. A global customer in Singapore would start fresh with IBM Singapore, and the IBM experience servicing that client in other countries would not be accessed. A European executive actually stopped Gerstner's e-mail from reaching employees, arguing that he had judged the e-mail inappropriate for his team and hard to translate. (His tenure with the firm after that incident was brief.) These silo groups often had their own ad agencies—there were over seventy, and there was virtually no cooperation among them. A major trade magazine carried fifteen IBM ads—each with its own message, look and feel, and even logo—in one month and no IBM presence in the next.

During the first year, IBM hired Abby Kohnstamm, a seasoned marketing executive with fourteen years at American Express. She got the attention of the worldwide management council, formed partly to move forward worldwide initiatives, by putting on a wall examples of ads, packaging, and collateral material. It was a mess—it was hard to argue that IBM could not do better. She then replaced the seventy-some ad agencies with a single agency, Ogilvy & Mather. A year later the company was in the field with an ad campaign showing that IBM was global and delivering integrated solutions to clients (the tagline: "Solutions for a Small Planet"). There was a dramatic change in the control and allocation of the communications budget. The silos, which had controlled 90 percent of the some $800 million budget, leaving only 10 percent for the support of the IBM brand, found their share reduced to 50 percent, a rather dramatic change.

Two years after Gerstner arrived, the silo organization was replaced with an industry-oriented organization with eleven industries (such as banking, government, and insurance) plus a small and medium business unit. This reorganization, which changed the way the firm thought and went to market, was highly disruptive and, according to Gerstner, took three years to gain real acceptance in the firm.

BBVA, one of the largest financial services firms in the world with some 7,500 branches (mostly in Spain and Latin America) and over 95,000 employees, reached its current size in part with a significant merger in 1999.[3] The CEO (who actually came from the smaller of the merged firms) was an entrepreneurial, change-oriented, forceful executive who initiated a brand strategy along with a program to centralize the direction of much of marketing. His initiatives were motivated by the need to reconcile the two major merged brands, a decline in customer satisfaction, and his belief that customer relationship needed to be a cornerstone of the bank's strategy going forward. A member of the executive committee and head of communication and image, Javier Ayuso, headed the effort.

The first step for BBVA was to create a common sense of corporate values, vision, and brand by getting input from employees, customers, and other stakeholders. In total, BBVA held over one hundred focus groups with customers from major segments, interviewed over one hundred thousand consumers, and conducted many in-depth interviews. As a result, the vision became "working for a better future for people"; the values centered on leadership, innovation, and focus on people; and the brand centered on the customer experience where the customer connects to the firm and its values. BBVA implemented the brand internally with brand engagement programs in which the top executives attended a three-day workshop. In eight-hour workshops, it then trained twenty thousand managers who then trained the rest of the firm. Externally, the branches were on a program to be redesigned, with their employees retrained. Two advertising agencies replaced the twenty-seven silo agencies. The company centralized the look and feel of the brand as well as the measures of performance and brand equity. It redirected the scattered sponsorship throughout Latin America toward a central theme of children's education.

An important aspect of getting buy-in throughout the organization was demonstrating the financial payoff of the new strategy and initiatives. Results showed that a 5 percent increase in employee commitment, for example, was associated with a 1.3 percent increase in client satisfaction and a 0.5 percent increase in sales. An impressive return on investment (ROI) and customer satisfaction were associated with changes in the branches.

In addition to the five roles just described, several dysfunctional roles or styles exist, which are described in the box. Unfortunately, they are not uncommon.

The Activity Scope and Authority

What activities should be within the purview of the CMO team? Within each activity, what role along the spectrum of facilitator to strategic captain should the CMO team play? Although there may be a dominant role, in general the role will vary not only over time and over silo, but over activity.

The following representative activities are potentially part of the CMO's charge. The first group, process activities, is associated with the facilitator role. The rest could be associated with any of the five roles. Even within one activity, the CMO team can sometimes play one role and, in other circumstances, play another.

- *Process activities.* Activities associated with the facilitator role could include, for example, establishing a common planning framework, organizing meetings and events to exchange information, creating networks and teams, and managing intranet sites including knowledge hubs.

- *Training and marketing talent upgrade.* The CMO team is the logical source of upgrading marketing talent throughout the firm. It could also, as at GE and IBM, be involved in identifying talent gaps and in career development. Training of marketing staff should often be centralized because it is common over silos.

- *Research and market insights.* The CMO team could take a leadership role in conducting cross-silo market research and driving toward customer insights. Several firms have a central "insight" group that develops insights that are relevant across silos.

- *Measurement.* The CMO team can be a vehicle to develop and support brand equity measurement across silos. The contribution

Dysfunctional Central Marketing Management Styles

To accomplish silo-spanning objectives, the CMO team must have or have access to brand, marketing, market, and product knowledge, organizational sensitivity, and adequate authority and resources. Efforts with the organization to proceed without one or more of these capabilities can result in one of the following:

- **Marketing bureaucracy.** The marketing group has marketing and brand knowledge but often lacks adequate market knowledge and is weak in organizational sensitivity and seriously deficient in authority and resources. The team becomes a logo cop charged with making sure that the visual presentation is correct, and perhaps with sending out forms to be filled in by the business units. The model can work for a while especially when the visual presentation is clearly confused and inconsistent. But over time the team has little real influence and is often ignored.

- **Big hat, no cattle.** This expression comes from Western movies where some cowboys with no resources talk big (and wear a "big" hat), while others with thousands of head of cattle talk softly. In this model, top management decides that marketing and brands are important. A team is created, sometimes with very capable people with marketing, brand, and market knowledge. However, little or no authority and resources are given, and organizational skills are weak. As a result, the team cannot influence autonomous

of the group would be to encourage as much commonality as possible in terms of the measures used for comparing brand performance over silos. It can also create tools to measure the performance of marketing programs.

business units, cannot hire outside experts, cannot really do anything that requires resources or authority. As a result, nothing gets done, and the organization gets frustrated or realizes that the top management really is only giving lip services to brands. This model too often occurs where the corporate brand dominates.

- **Uninformed dictator.** In this model, a person with organizational power, sometimes the CEO, becomes convinced that brand is a key asset and must be strengthened, and for whatever reason, does not delegate the job to the CMO, perhaps because there is no CMO or no empowered CMO. This sometimes-reborn brand champion, however, lacks knowledge of branding, marketing, markets, and/or products and, most importantly, patience. As a result, he or she is prone to make arbitrary decisions without research or analysis. Perhaps, for example, this person makes a hasty and arbitrary decision to standardize the brand name or position without a strategy or much analysis. The result could be a disastrous erosion of local market positions, employee buy-in, and organizations' ability to coordinate silos going forward.

- **Anarchy.** In the anarchy model, the organization has an extremely decentralized structure and culture. Either there is no central marketing team, or it has so little scope and authority, that it can only observe silos do their thing. There may be local market knowledge, but if marketing or brand knowledge exists, it is probably uneven and sprinkled through the organization. Some business units will do well, but the organization as a whole will be underleveraged, and the brand will tend to be confusing to the customer.

- *Functional specialist.* The CMO team could provide services to those silos that lack expertise in functional marketing areas such as advertising, the Internet, or sponsorship.

- *Visual presentation guidelines.* Often a motivation for creating a central brand group is the visible fact that the brand's visual presentation across business units is inconsistent, and it is clear to everyone that some central coordination could provide relatively cheap, fast, and painless dividends.

- *Corporate marketing programs.* Having the CMO team in charge of a corporate marketing program such as corporate advertising, a global sponsorship such as the Olympics, or a firmwide Web site would help insure that the coordination across silos needed to maximize the program's impact would be in place.

- *Brand strategy.* A central vehicle to coordinate silos and create synergies is the brand strategy for those firms with brand-sharing silos. The need is to get agreement on what the brand should stand for and to understand how the brand must be adapted to silo contexts so that it remains consistent not only to the market but also internally. A strong, coherent brand should drive all the marketing programs.

- *Marketing programs.* A host of marketing programs can have a cross-silo component such as:
  - Advertising
  - Promotions
  - Sponsorships
  - PR
  - Packaging
  - Call centers

One issue is the level of control and involvement of the local silo groups. A related issue is whether the CMO team can and should be the source of ideas for programs. Being an R&D shop for ideas can fill a vacuum in organizations in which most are involved in day-to-day activities. An alternative is to have the group react to and exploit ideas created within the countries.

- *Digital marketing.* Because digital marketing, including social technology, is both important and confusingly dynamic, a centralized, core competence in the area can be a key asset. Consider, for example, the varied forms of Internet-based advertising such as viral ads (ads that use existing social networks), the webisode (a short sitcom episode with a branded message), consumer-generated ads, and the long-form interactive (a viral campaign that draws viewers in for weeks at a time).

- *Integrated marketing.* Most firms have major brand-building efforts and other marketing initiatives involving vehicles such as advertising, sponsorship, and PR that are organizationally or functionally independent from one another. As a result, inconsistency and a failure to gain overall synergy are inevitable. The CMO team may be well suited to develop organizational units that will further integrated marketing communication (IMC) and even to coordinate these efforts.

- *Innovation.* Bringing marketing research, customer insights, and market-testing expertise to the table, the CMO team can be actively involved in innovation for new products, product improvements, or marketing programs. In several firms, such as GE and P&G, the CMO takes on a strategic partner role in the innovation initiatives of the firm.

- *The brand portfolio.* The CMO team is often the only entity that has the perspective to analyze and manage the brand portfolio. What should be the identity and position of brands that cross silos? What are their roles? Can brands be leveraged? Can brand synergy be created or enhanced? Can discipline in the naming of new offerings be imposed so that new brand names are created only when justified and when they fit portfolio goals?

- *Alliances.* Business strategy often relies heavily on alliances because needed assets to be successful in a product market are missing. For example, a global brand is sometimes not welcome or too costly to establish in a country, and access to a local brand through an alliance may be a way to create local credibility and distribution quickly and efficiently. The CMO team can facilitate such alliances and make sure they are compatible with the total brand portfolio strategy.

- *M&A activities.* The CMO team could evaluate potential M&A candidates when significant brand issues are often ignored or assumed away. They could also address the brand portfolio issues after the transaction is made. At GE over the years, the CMO did have such a role in part because the CMO was seasoned, comfortable with finance and strategy, and close to the CEO.

- *Resource allocation.* Allocating brand-building resources among the silo entities is sensitive because the organizational units usually believe that the profits they earn are theirs to invest. However, gross misallocations of marketing resources often occur from an organizational perspective. The ability of the CMO team to make observations about the allocation judgments, if not actually control them, could dramatically improve both short-term performance and strategic prospects.

- *Seat at the strategy table.* The ultimate influence of the CMO is to have a seat at the executive table when business strategy issues are addressed. For this to happen, the firm must accept brand equity as a strategic asset and the brand portfolio as a strategy enabler, and have confidence in the experience and insight of the CMO.

Although there will usually be a dominant CMO role, it can vary through activities. So the CMO team can be a facilitator when helping country teams develop brand plans, a consultant when helping them develop brand-building programs, and a strategic captain when enforcing the visual presentation of the brand.

UBS uses all three styles in different contexts—a facilitator role in creating marketing strategies, a consultative role in developing brand strategy, and a strategic captain role in developing a coherent brand portfolio and sponsorship strategy. The management of regional and global sponsorships, in particular, uses a strategic captain role. With respect to sponsorship evaluation, the CMO team makes go/no-go decisions, establishes measurable goals, validates themes from a brand view, makes sure the sponsorships are not duplicating, ensures that adequate support is available at the local level, and provides strategic input into the evaluation process. With respect to implementation, the CMO team negotiates the contract, provides funds for the rights, and develops an implementation plan that crosses countries. The country teams implement local activities to support the sponsorship and contribute local funds for exploitation activities. With respect to measurement, the central marketing team establishes a sponsorship peer review process, measures the impact of the sponsorship, and decides whether to continue it, while the local team provides data input and participates in the review process.

The role within an activity can evolve. At Visa, the CMO, playing a strategic captain role, initiated a global tracking study with a single vendor. After the tracking program was established, the CMO team became facilitators to keep the program running smoothly and consultants to add methodology and insights to the data analysis. The regional research people took over ownership and added some variants to the scales and their own vendors.

The level of autonomy that is appropriate for the silo marketing group with respect to activities and marketing programs is detailed in chapter 7. The CMO's activities and programs can be an imperative, making the silo marketing teams implementers; adaptable, where the silo teams have some leeway; and discretionary, whereby the silos have full control of the budget and programs.

What dictates what CMO team role is optimal for what activity? What level of silo autonomy is appropriate? A more aggressive role for the CMO team will be appropriate when, as previously noted, a firm and visible CEO commitment exists, marketing talent is available, there is a clear business vision that provides a compelling reason to reduce silo power, a sense of crises exists, and a change agent CMO is in place. In addition, other considerations when making the role decision at the activity level are discussed in chapter 7. They include the talent residing in the silos to support the activity, the nature and quality of the programs developed by the CMO team, how unique the silo contexts are, and the degree of organizational stress that will be generated by imposing programs on silo teams.

The Product and Country Scope

The assumption so far has been that the CMO will operate at the level of the total organization. However, the locus of CMO power is sometimes more appropriate at the level of a grouping of countries into regions or a grouping of products into categories.

Figure 1-2 shows an organization in the form of a product/country matrix (or more generally, a product/market matrix) that provides a way to visually structure the grouping decision. What subset of the product set shown in the figure should be the province of the CMO? Should it be a category of products, such as the computer products of HP? What countries? Should it be a region, such as Asia, Europe, the Americas, Africa, and the Middle East? The general question is, what should be ag-

FIGURE 1-2

The product/country matrix

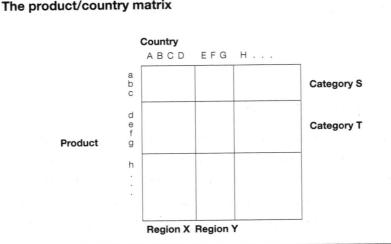

gregated? Too little, and the whole point of an integrative CMO is vitiated. Too much, and it can become unmanageable, with needed market and product knowledge missing. At what point should synergy and coordination occur?

A regional organization is sometimes the best vehicle to exert more aggressive strategy roles across the countries in part because a regional unit will be more likely to overcome the language and culture problems and will probably appear more credible to the country teams. Further, the practical matter of meeting and networking is best done regionally. A global unit may find the task of actively influencing country silos simply overwhelming.

Canon is organized into four regions, each of which is highly autonomous with respect to planning processes, brand strategy, and marketing programs. The result is very distinct, although not necessarily inconsistent, brand efforts. For example, the advertising tagline reflecting the brand position is "You Can Canon" in Europe, "Delighting You Always" in Asia, "Make It Possible with Canon" in Japan, and "Image Anywhere" in the United States. However, each region has a strong, centrally controlled marketing group with budget and program control of the country groups. The budget authority is central to the ability of the regional office to direct the efforts of the country teams. This regional influence represents an evolution from a more countrycentric organization that occurred in 2002.

Similarly, grouping products may be optimal when a firm has a wide range of products that is impractical to manage. Recall that during the 1980s P&G moved from managing brands to managing groups of brands that fit into a logical category. However, each category, such as skin care, hair care, and fabric care, is autonomous. The fabric care category (Tide, Era, Downy, Gain, etc.), for example, is a unit responsible for all the brands and products within the category, and has the authority to allocate innovations and brand-building resources over hair care brands and manage strategically their positioning in the silo marketplaces.

What is the best level of aggregation? Should the organization unit be country based, regional, or global? Should it involve a single product, a product grouping, or all products? Looking forward, should that orientation change? Basically, the analysis should look for the presence or absence of brand and program synergies, market synergies, management synergies, business model synergies, and scale synergies.

- *Brand and program synergies.* To what extent will the groups of products or countries share brands and marketing programs? The CMO scope should be affected by the potential for brand and program synergy. Contexts in which brand position synergy is unlikely; included are such considerations as differences in market share position (Toyota is much weaker in Europe than in the United States) and image (HP is not known as a printer company in Japan) is described in chapter 5. What grouping of products and/or countries will encourage the synergy potential to emerge?

- *Market synergies.* How much market overlap exists among the grouped product or country silos? Do customers get exposed to other silo business units? Are the products complementary—used together? Or do they appear in the same channels, so that exposure to one affects another? Do customers travel beyond the country in ways that are relevant for the offering? Is this travel predominately regional or global? Even in financial services the number of globetrotters is limited, while the number of regional travelers in Europe or Southeast Asia is more significant.

- *Management synergies.* What span of control is optimal? If it is too wide, it may affect the ability to manage effectively. If the products are so technical and so different or the countries are so distinct with subtle nuances that are critical to success, then it may be unwise to aggregate. The span of control interacts with the expected role of the CMO. If the CMO role is primarily a facilitator, consultant, and service provider, then a broader span of control will be feasible. Finally, there is the likely success of the assigned roles for the CMO team to consider. Will the CMO team have the capacity to gain the necessary product and market knowledge, depth of marketing talent, and CEO support to be effective?

- *Business model synergies.* There is also a business model perspective. To what extent is the same business model being employed across silos? For Fidelity Investments, countries outside the United States are accessed through third-party agents, a model very different from that of the United States, making a global brand effort less appropriate. An oil company may need to divide the convenience store from the retail gasoline business and even lubes (motor oil) from gasoline, and have a CMO for each of the three because the business model is so different.

- *Scale synergies.* There is also the practical issue of scale. If a silo business is large and important, it might justify its own CMO team that can focus on its unique context, including its brand image and distribution channel, even though that creates a significant silo barrier. That is the case for Toyota in the United States or the home market of Shiseido or Visa. A single product category, such as the printer business of HP, requires its own central marketing team. Conversely, a silo business that is too small to support a CMO team will necessarily have to be grouped with other silos even if it has unique characteristics. Ford, in Europe, must aggregate smaller countries out of practical necessity.

Executives should recognize that there will be a silo-driven bias toward a low level of aggregation. The silos will argue (and believe) that the synergies will not exist, be smaller than expected, or be associated with excessive cost in resources, closeness to customer, and decisiveness. This, of course, is the classic case for silos in the first place.

Often, two or more levels of groupings will be involved. A product could be managed by region but also globally with a regional CMO and a global CMO. There could be a product marketing manager for one product, such as HP's LaserJet, and a category manager for all of HP's printer products. The roles of the CMOs or marketing managers in each level can differ, and differ by activity. So the good news is that there is a lot of room to maneuver. The bad news is that there is a lot of room to maneuver. The resulting flexibility will tend to aid the cause of silo re-sistance to central marketing.

When there are multiple CMO teams covering multiple product or country groupings, there is usually a role for a corporate CMO as well, but a different one as is evidenced in three large firms. At P&G the corporate CMO is in charge of corporate marketing with a relatively modest budget, but works to upgrade the competence within the organization of the marketing disciplines, especially those that are emerging, and plays an influential facilitator and consultant role in the silo groups. At Dell part of the corporate CMO's job is to coordinate the communication firms with the objective to gain efficiencies and improved consistencies. At GE one of the corporate CMO tasks is to run the firmwide innovation initiatives.

For Discussion

1. In your firm, what is the dominant role of the CMO? What should it be?

2. What is the role of the CMO in each of the activities listed? What should it be?

3. How are the products grouped? Is that optimal?

4. How are the countries grouped? Is that optimal?

Chapter 2

Gain Credibility and Buy-in

Focus on metrics. Do it for your own personal credibility.

—James Stengel, chief marketing officer, Procter & Gamble[1]

A journey of a thousand miles begins with a single step.

—Confucius

CREDIBILITY is the key to CMO success at breaking down silo barriers and fostering cooperation and synergy. Without mutual respect, without an atmosphere where silos include or seek out the CMO's team, progress on cross-silo issues will be slow. No matter how much authority the CEO has granted the CMO, the silos will avoid, ignore, or even ridicule the CMO team's efforts if its actions cause credibility to fade.

Gaining credibility, the first milestone of the CMO team, usually meets resistance from the silos whose autonomy, a source of personal fulfillment and pride, is threatened. They fear that the resulting constraints will lead to less effective marketing, marketing for which they are held accountable. In addition, they sense the coming of such burdens as meetings and rules that will, at best, cost time and resources and accomplish nothing.

How can a CMO gain credibility and buy-in to initiatives? This chapter introduces five routes (see figure 2-1). The first section discusses ways to get the CEO on board. The second presents the power of customer knowledge. The third talks about the influence of visible successes, even small ones. The fourth argues that respecting and engaging the silo teams is one key to success. The final section covers the basic concept of staffing the central marketing group with credible people.

Gaining CEO Support—A Key to Success

In the 1980s a perfect storm occurred at Intel. A gifted brand strategist, Dennis Carter, was directing strategy with the side-by-side partnership of a CEO, Andy Grove, who fundamentally understood brands and their importance to business strategy. In the early 1990s, they jointly launched the centrally run "Intel Inside" program, which dominated the marketing budget and, indeed, the company business strategy. Intel Inside was followed by an innovation stream supported by brands like Pentium and a coherent, resourced brand strategy. In the Intel scheme the CMO was

FIGURE 2-1

Routes to credibility and buy-in

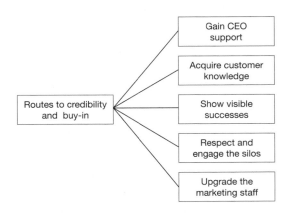

a strategic captain role and the silos implemented the strategy. This branding success would not have happened without an involved, enlightened CEO. Few CMOs are blessed with a brand strategy so closely linked to a business strategy and a CEO like Andy Grove. Most have to bring the CEO along—sometimes a long way.

CMO success will be affected by the level of support from the CEO. Even with the facilitator role, the CMO will need authority and resources to pursue initiatives. The challenge is to gain visible CEO support, if not involvement. The CEO must believe that marketing is a priority and be willing to support strategically sound marketing programs with authority and resources. That means more than token lip service without substance; it means an ongoing commitment that will not falter at the first stress point. One central marketing team laughed when I asked whether its budget was adequate—members laughed because the budget was always adequate in January and always disappeared in September to "make the numbers."

The most effective strategy to get a CEO on board will depend on the context and the CEO's style and priorities, but four approaches have worked and should be considered: to reframe marketing, to measure performance, to enlist the assistance of the CFO and others, and to involve the CEO.

Reframe Marketing

Change the way marketing is perceived in the organization by aligning its role with that of the priority agenda. Focus on growth objectives instead of brand extensions, on efficiency and cost objectives instead of marketing synergy or scale, and on building assets to support strategic initiatives instead of brand image campaigns. The objective is to reframe marketing as strategic, a driver of the business strategy, instead of being a tactical management function. The goal is to avoid the CMO's being positioned as another functional area advocate (every slot needs more resources).

The perception that marketing is not aligned with the CEO agenda is too common. In a 2004 survey of nearly four hundred executives from one hundred companies conducted by the ANA (Association of National

Advertisers) and Booz Allen Hamilton one finding was that over half the companies were perceived as failing to have alignment of marketing with CEO priorities.[2]

Measure Performance

Use hard numbers in showing the relationship between marketing and financial performance. When the CMO teams can demonstrate an attractive ROI or its absence, it enhances their stature and at least reduces their image of being soft and unanalytical. In this era of financial accountability, the C-suite team is often uncomfortable when performance is not measured.

Demonstrating performance is not easy. Time series data over silos is expensive and creates issues such as what to measure when. Even when it exists, there is often inadequate variation in marketing programs to sort out effectiveness. Field experimentation is expensive, assumes that there are marketing programs in "final form" ready to test, and creates delays in implementing programs. Further, many marketing programs are likely to have an effect over a long time, which makes ROI estimates more difficult.

However difficult the task, measuring performance must be a priority for the CMO team. In the short run, the team should exploit the existing data and pursue opportunities for experimentation. Developing a few field experiments within the silo world can show the value of quantifying performance. In the long run, the CMO team should seek to own or be an influence to two initiatives. The first is to develop strong cross-silo market tracking data along with measures of the size and loyalty of customer segments that can reflect the long-term impact of marketing programs. The second is to develop an ongoing program of experimentation that supports the refinement of existing marketing programs and the creation of new ones.

Chevron is one firm that goes overboard in developing empirical measures of the brand and the results of marketing programs such as sponsorships. The Chevron CMO team recognizes that the culture is data driven and it is helpful to be on the same page. Data that can be linked to profitability is especially persuasive. In that context, new programs that are field tested and can generate estimates of short-term and long-term ROI will have a strong argument.

Enlist Allies

A CEO is used to having direct reports advocate for their area. It can be persuasive, therefore, for a more neutral spokesperson to carry the CMO's message, and even better if that person has the CEO's ear. The CMO has several natural allies in the executive suite. The CFO can understand that marketing can both influence the long-term success of the firm's strategy and affect the budget by showing how to do more with less by reducing the inefficiencies that silo barriers create. The head of HR can see the value of a strong brand with an internal brand-building program to help build a consistent culture. The head of sales can advocate for synergistic programs between sales and marketing.

Involve the CEO

The CEO, indeed the entire top management team, can be involved in creating parts of the marketing strategy, such as determining the brand vision. MasterCard nominated a six-member executive brand board to support and advise its brand-building program, from product offerings to advertising, to major sponsorships. Nestlé has each of its top executives also serve as a champion for a major brand. 3M created a top-level group to approve all new brand names, resulting in a dramatic reduction in brand proliferation and focusing attention on the power of the master brands in the portfolio. Sony's CEO acts as de facto CMO. When the CEO is intimately involved, the needed support and resources are more likely to be forthcoming.

There is often a tipping point, at which the CEO who was a spectator becomes engaged. That often occurs when the current brand assets do not adequately support a new business strategy. Brand strategy, as a result, becomes a priority, the CEO gets involved in making it happen, and the autonomy of the silos gets reviewed. Several firms, such as Schlumberger and UBS, for example, have decided that the service offering needed more of an integrated, team approach. As a result, the CEO in each case championed the repositioning of the corporate brand and its elevation to the prime flag-carrying role at the expense of the prior silo brands, such as Schlumberger's Anadrill or UBS's Warburg.

When the tipping point occurs and CEO-driven brand and marketing momentum is created, a one-time opportunity exists to change the role of central marketing. At UBS the new strategy and the elevation of the UBS brand, which now spanned the silos, made central control of marketing more logical and reduced resistance to change because such resistance would imply a failure to buy into the new strategy. The central marketing group capitalized by obtaining budget and strategic responsibility for materially all brand advertising and sponsorship across the firm, not just corporate advertising and sponsorship. For sponsorship, for example, the CMO team, as noted in chapter 1, now develops a sponsorship strategy, makes go/no-go decisions, establishes measurable goals, negotiates the contracts, and proposes implementation plans that cross countries. The local business units implement and fund local activities to support and exploit the sponsorship. These changes, which ultimately enabled the new business strategy, could never have happened at any other time in the life of the firm.

Acquiring Customer Knowledge

The ultimate source of influence is customer knowledge. "The customer is telling us that . . ." is a powerful and hard-to-refute argument. When the CMO team has a better grasp of the customer than the silos do, or at least has the same level of customer understanding, the discussions can proceed without the "you do not understand this market" overlay. Having firsthand knowledge of a segmentation study, ethnographic research, satisfaction research, or tracking data will create credibility. If the CMO inputs are based on the emergence of a new segment, a new application, a systematic dissatisfaction with the product, or a declining brand, they will be hard to ignore.

The service supplier role, in which the CMO team becomes the go-to place for research methods, can provide a way to gain customer knowledge. Controlling the customer research, for example, means that the CMO team at least has access to the customer information. If the CMO team contributed to the analysis and interpretation of ethnographic studies, for example, there will be a depth of understanding that affects the relationship with the silos. Philips, a global maker of consumer electronics, lighting, and personal care products, created a centralized consumer intelligence unit that was responsible for conducting consumer research and tracking and measuring the Philips brand across regions. The output allowed the central group to generate customer insights and make comparative judgments.

A way to create depth in customer knowledge is to form teams within the central marketing group that focus on a market trend, customer segment, emerging application, or another timely topic relating to the customer. The team can represent a "center of excellence" and affect the ability of the CMO team to contribute to strategy discussions.

Getting out in the field is still another approach. A. G. Lafley, before he became CEO, was the head of P&G Asia. In one of his first visits to Japan in that capacity, he was told by the cosmetics manager in Japan that cosmetics is nothing like laundry detergents, where Lafley had achieved success.[3] After spending a month talking to customers at sales counters and in homes, Lafley could conclude that, in fact, cosmetics is very much like detergents—it is all about understanding customers, going beyond what they articulate, and delighting them with products. His firsthand knowledge of customers qualitatively changed the nature of his interaction with the cosmetics team and later led to the introduction of one of P&G's most successful skin care products.

As CEO, Lafley encourages everyone in marketing to spend time with customers. Such "immersion research" involves "living it" by being with customers as they use the product, "shopping it" by being with them during the shopping experience, and "working it" by being a salesperson who helps them make decisions.

Showing Success Visibly

Nothing succeeds like success. Demonstrating success is perhaps the best way to gain credibility and buy-in. A program credited to the CMO team that works will attract people who will associate themselves with it. They will explicitly or vicariously become part of the team. Further, a case study that becomes a role model can be very influential because people understand specific role models.

A marketing program, to be recognized as successful, has to be both persuasive and visible. A key to persuasiveness is measurement. At Adobe a key phrase is *demonstrated value*. If a program cannot demonstrate its value, it is unlikely to be funded. Demonstrating value on the basis of market tests and time series measures will impress not only the CEO but the whole organization—as long as it is communicated. Active communication using a variety of personal and internal media will often be needed. The success must become well known in the silo world to be influential in moving the CMO team up the credibility scale.

Success can come in many forms. One can be the quick wins, modest programs that the CMO's team can implement in a short time horizon. These are *singles* in baseball parlence. Another type is the program with major impact—the *home run*. Each has its place in gaining credibility.

Getting Easy Wins

A host of problems and issues will confront any CMO, especially a new or newly empowered one. With limited time, resources, and organizational tolerance, the CMO must give a few important issues priority in attention and resources. However, the CMO also needs to generate visible wins by finding opportunities to generate quick results that will enhance the credibility of the CMO team. Five questions can help locate potential quick-hit opportunities.

First, which element of the marketing effort is obviously deficient and would require modest resources to fix? If the problem is widely recognized, little effort will be required to make the case for change. Further, improvements will probably be easy to realize. The visual brand display of the various silos (logos, layouts, look and feel, symbols, etc.) on a large wall is often in this category—recall that IBM used that technique to make visible the inconsistency with which the IBM brand was portrayed in its many silos. Dell does this in the presence of the CEO on a regular basis to make sure that any inconsistencies are identified and dealt with.

CIGNA has a service council that uncovered the fact that letters being sent to customers used legalese and did not even have a phone number, despite requesting that the customer call within twenty-four hours if there was a problem. An effort to improve was obviously needed and provided a measurable, visible win for the marketing group that had the improvement of customer touch points as a priority.

Second, what silo units are eager for help with serious marketing problems affecting performance? Perhaps their local brands are inadequate for the market context. Or perhaps critical promotional dollars are ineffective or being wasted. The more desperate the organizational unit, the better, as long as silo management is receptive to help. Look for silos who are grasping for solutions and who are motivated to be cooperative and involved in implementing any program. At one electronics firm, a group focusing on the home market was in trouble because the brand was deficient in that context; it was perceived as too "corporate" even though other organizational units focusing on business users were doing fine. The home products group was eager for help in overcoming its liability by repositioning and repackaging its product. At MasterCard, the Latin American group welcomed help, whereas the Pacific regional team was isolationist; its CEO wanted to stamp passports—not a direction for easy wins.

Third, what programs can the CMO introduce "under the radar," in that they can be done without approval? For example, at CIGNA, the real estate manager, who needed artwork for a building, was persuaded to use brand visuals. The CEO of a major division saw the result and promptly decided to extend the idea to all the buildings. The idea may not have survived a typical presentation to the CEO. At Hitachi, a big win occurred when the CMO consolidated the six booths at a major trade show into one. The impact of both these initiatives was visible and provided a step toward building credibility for the central marketing group.

Fourth, what marketing factors cross business units? At BP, the CMO's team searches for commonalities across silos. What functional expertise or database would multiple silos use? Could the CMO team develop that expertise so that they would be the go-to source and thus would be invited to the marketing strategy table as a result? Activities such as segmentation studies or ethnographic research are candidates. The marketing group could also look to programs that by their nature will span silos and may require funding that would not be viable for an individual silo. Programs like these, such as the MasterCard World Cup sponsorship, can be a vehicle to get the silo groups to work together and form relationships.

Fifth, what are the priority initiatives of the CEO, and what doable marketing programs would advance those priorities? Such programs would have the potential to influence the strategic credibility of the CMO team, a key long-term asset. The CMO team at GE has contributed to the environmentally sensitive innovation that is the backbone of the GE business strategy which has been given the umbrella brand "ecomagination." A later chapter will elaborate.

It is remarkable what visible success can do to the credibility of the CMO team, even if that success is not material. Success breeds success. Jim Collins, in his book *Good to Great*, talks about the flywheel effect in describing how good companies become great through incremental tangible accomplishments.[4] A huge flywheel weighing thousands of pounds would be difficult to get started. The first few revolutions would require a lot of effort, but gradually the flywheel would rotate faster and faster. After hundreds of revolutions, the same effort used to start the movement would be adding speed because the task would be to build on the enormous momentum of the unit. There would be no way to determine which push created the momentum, because they all did in their small way. Creating a series of small victories that are associated with the CMO team has the potential, if properly managed, to foster momentum that can be hard to stop—the flywheel effect.

Delivering Real Impact—The Home Run

John F. Kennedy, after the disastrous attempt to invade Cuba at the Bay of Pigs, observed that "success has many fathers but failure is an orphan." It is easy to gain not only credibility and buy-in but involvement for a program that achieves excellence. Everyone wants to be a part of, indeed take some credit for, a compelling idea. Delivering a successful program is the ultimate driver of credibility, more than even the best credentials. But the program has to be truly outstanding. Good is not good enough, and mediocre can be terminal.

Creating a marketing or brand initiative or program that achieves excellence is easy to say and hard to do, of course. Methods to generate home run marketing programs that leverage the silo organization will be discussed in chapter 7. There are many potential avenues, from major sponsorships to digital marketing, to events, to advertising campaigns. The trick is to find one that can carry the banner of the CMO team.

One source of a home run idea when a master brand spans silos is the brand vision. The brand vision is a key part of the CMO's portfolio and a driver of most of the other potential initiatives. If it clicks, reflects a compelling strategy, resonates with customers, and inspires the employees, it can energize the organization, including the CEO, and legitimize other marketing initiatives. That is especially true when the team successfully involves the CEO in creating the vision. When the CEO endorses the vision and carries the message internally, the path becomes smoother, and the ability of the CMO and his or her team to directly sponsor initiatives and deal with silo issues is much enhanced.

A host of cases have occurred in which a brand vision supporting a CEO-sponsored strategic direction was so inspiring and compelling that it empowered the CMO to make a dramatic difference.

Consider General Electric. Jeffrey Immelt, who arrived in 2003, decided that organic growth around innovation was to be the business strategy going forward, and the CMO team would be central in the new direction. The team replaced the venerable slogan "We bring good things to life" with "imagination at work," a concept that resonated with employees and customers. The CMO's team also was the manager of the flagship internal program to generate new business areas, termed *imagination breakthroughs*; the leader of four cross-business teams; and in charge of selling the new vision to the organization.

Achieving excellence can mean some tough calls because just as success can breed success, failure can breed failure. At UBS at one time, a major advertising campaign was not projected by judgment and in testing to be outstanding. As a result, the CMO team made a painful decision to start over, even though that involved budget and schedule deadlines. The end result was a compelling campaign that helped represent the brand story around the "You and us" theme that spoke about the personal attention available and worked across the varied target markets. If the team had not been persistent in the face of time pressures, they would have missed not only achieving market success but also a huge uptick in their credibility.

Respecting and Engaging the Silo Units

By relying on authority, the CMO risks appearing arbitrary and arrogant and stimulating the natural resentment and avoidance schemes that silos are only too good at. While it is crucial to have the support and delegated authority of the CEO, it is equally crucial to avoid using it but, rather, have it in the shadows, a silent incentive to cooperate. The CMO still must earn legitimacy by insights, actions, and results.

At the outset, one priority for the CMO should be to listen, to learn the pain points of the silo teams in both their business and their link to central marketing. Not only will a listening program provide crucial inputs, but it will also signal that the interaction going forward will be based on respect and open future communication channels.

Another early priority is to develop relationships. The top marketing officer of Google is one of many who indicated that personal relationships are the key to dealing with silo issues. The optimum is to have a partner relationship where the CMO is seen as supporting and enhancing silo performance rather than being seen as an authoritative, bureaucratic, negative force. Having one-way impersonal communication dominate the relationship is a recipe for failure.

Even in the role of creating and enforcing visual guidelines, the goal should be to have clear guidelines and to partner rather than be a logo cop. When the guidelines do not cover a situation, getting involved at the right time is one key. When the name and visual design are being developed (rather than after that has been done and "permission" is sought), for example, constructive teaming can occur, which can prevent the emergence of an "off-brand" direction.

As the CMO team matures and the organization develops initiatives, skills in selling them versus forcing them on the silos becomes important. Progress will be faster when the silo teams recognize the value of the CMO initiatives. The CMO team should make the rationale as well as the content clear. Internal marketing of the brand vision, discussed further in a later chapter, can provide a platform for selling the overall strategy.

It is helpful if the silo units feel that they were part of the creation of the strategy as well as the implementation. One firm makes it a point to include the relevant cross-silo team in some of the glamorous parts of developing the advertising campaign, to make the silo involvement more interesting. The silo people even visit the ad creation sessions to get a close-up feel for the process. Involving silo management leads to market insights, buy-in, and more effective local implementation.

One way to avoid the silo units' feeling like outsiders is to disperse the central marketing team. Coca-Cola, for example, headquarters its Sprite brand in Hong Kong because much of the growth and innovation for Sprite is in Asia. Lycra, a thirty-five-year-old ingredient brand from DuPont, delegates the marketing leadership responsibility for each of its major applications to a country with some link to that application— the Brazilian marketing manager is also the global lead for swimsuits; the French marketing manager does the same for fashion; and so on. A financial services company located some of the functional groups, such as marketing research and brand strategy, in different countries. Such dispersion sends a signal that the central marketing group truly spans silos without a "headquarters"-centric model.

The CMO charged with creating or enhancing the coordination between the silos must carefully balance the needs of the silo units with programs to centralize. The silos should have the necessary flexibility to succeed in their marketplace. If that is arbitrarily removed, they not only will be handicapped but may be resentful and withhold the collaborative attitude that is needed. The goal of the CMO should not be to centralize all marketing people, budgets, decisions, and programs. It is rather to create effective, efficient marketing programs, strong brands in all markets, and market success everywhere. Later chapters discuss conditions under which to adapt the master brand to local markets and more specific guidelines for allocating authority to the silo units.

Upgrading the Marketing Staff

It is the people who make it happen. The right people can probably make virtually any system work, and the wrong people can make the most "optimal" system fail. Creating the right team sends a powerful signal to the organization. Who is added, and even more important, who is asked to leave will be closely observed. Adding people who are respected can give the group a lift, while retaining people who do not fit the role can be debilitating.

Skills Needed

The qualifications that the CMO team needs are extraordinary. Collectively, the group must be knowledgeable about marketing, branding, markets, products, and their organization. In addition, the group must have a strategic perspective and be collaborative, persuasive, a change agent, and, for a global firm, multicultural. The CMO needs to seek people who have as many of these characteristics as possible:

- *Knowledgeable.* An effective central marketing management team needs to collectively have a breadth of knowledge. Achieving that breadth can involve a mix of generalists with insight, specialists, and outside resources, but it must create competence in the following:

- Marketing knowledge—marketing strategy and programs, segmentation, measurement, communication vehicles and, critically, the new media

- Brand knowledge—brands, brand power, brand equity, brand roles, brand portfolio strategy, and brand-building programs

- Market knowledge—markets, country cultures, market trends, competitor dynamics, customer segmentation, and customer motivation

- Product knowledge—product or service attributes and the underlying technology, plus the innovation flow that will define future products and services

- Organizational knowledge—the organization, its culture, strategies, values, and formal and informal influence and communication structure

The required level of authority or resources and knowledge of marketing, brands, markets, products, and the organization will depend on the roles employed. The strategic partner and captain roles require extremely high levels of each. If one is not sufficient, suboptimal options and decisions will be inevitable. The consultant role is a bit less demanding because the local managers will control the ultimate inputs and decisions. However, even the facilitator role, the least demanding, will still work best if the levels are high, although market and product knowledge can reside at the silo level as long as the facilitator role is accepted.

- *Strategic perspective.* The CMO team should be able to strategize, to move beyond being proficient in a set of tactics to being involved in marketing strategy. Because the team members will be dealing with a dynamic marketplace, they will also need to be comfortable with adapting strategy to reflect those dynamics. Without a strategic flare, the team will not be capable of devising cross-silo marketing strategies, which should be a major goal, and will not be a candidate to sit at the strategy table. The strategic perspective should be grounded in analytical decision making linked to the world of the CFO.

- *Collaborative.* Those on the CMO team, as well as key silo marketing people, need to be collaborative, especially when the incentives are silo oriented. In fact, they need to be part of the effort to create or reinforce a collaborative organizational culture. At IBM, being collaborative is part of the evaluation criteria; the goal is to have people who have a real desire to learn about the products, operations, and programs of other business units and an ability to work across silos. In fact, top central marketing people at IBM evaluate not only the central marketing team on this dimension but also the silo marketing people. At Allstate, the CMO's leadership team must be able (and willing) to operate in a highly collaborative, free-flowing environment where "positive confrontation" is welcomed. These people need to be receptive to stress-testing and improving ideas rather than disregarding or opposing them. They have to move on if they require excessive rules and guidelines.

- *Persuasive.* The CMO team needs at least some members to be persuaders, to have communication and leadership skills. Communication should go beyond presentations to an ability to understand and communicate to an audience in their terms. And leadership extends communication to inspiration, to get others to buy in to the fundamental mission or objective. Even the most compelling vision and the most effective programs require selling. Most of the observed CMO successes were associated with the CMO and others' traveling the silos with the message of a new strategy while at the same time building relationships.

- *Change agent.* Most CMOs need to be a change agent. That means being able to generate the feeling and substance of being creative and innovative. The team should not only come up with ideas, but, perhaps more important, recognize and support new ideas from silo teams with encouragement, empowerment, and resources.

A sense of energy and purpose should exist. Life will not go on as before. Change will happen. There is a fine line, however, between being a loose cannon and a positive catalyst for change. The change message should be surrounded by professionalism.

- *Multicultural.* When the global overlay is added, the ability to work with different languages and cultures becomes a requirement. Particularly in a culturally homogeneous country like Japan—and even the United States, where few are proficient in other languages—it is necessary to build a team that is culturally sensitive with adequate language skills. One route, used by Schlumberger, the oil field services firm, is to deliberately source the whole firm with nationals from around the world. The result is one of the few companies that can say they are truly multicultural. Another route is to rotate people around the globe, as Nestlé and Sony do, creating the absence of country-specific people. Still another is to explicitly train people in cultural knowledge, market insights, and so on to reduce their limitations. But being multicultural will remain a challenge for the firm with global aspirations.

Sourcing People

A basic decision is whether the CMO and his or her staff members should be outsiders or insiders. There is usually a sharp trade-off. The insider will be more likely to know the organization, its culture, and systems; will have a network of colleagues to tap into for information and help in designing and implementing programs; and will know the actors behind the formal organization chart—who are the real keys to getting things done. The insider will thus be low risk. However, the insider may lack marketing skills and credibility and may refuse or fail to adopt a change agent role because it is organizationally and personally uncomfortable.

An outsider with the needed marketing skills and credibility can serve as a change agent in part because he or she is less tied to past decisions, relationships, and political pressures. The problem is that he or she will often be flying blind internally without the benefit of an established network throughout the firm to draw on. This is the riskier route but one that might be more likely to make a difference when the organization is in need of change. The risk goes up when the outsider is changing industries (e.g., from packaged goods to B2B marketing) and facing new and different marketing challenges.

The trade-offs between the inside and the outside source suggest staffing routes. An insider with a proven record as a change agent who has or could obtain credibility in marketing and brands may be available. Or an outsider who has demonstrated an ability to adapt to organizations may be a target. Sequencing the marketing manager is possible as well. An insider might get started and gain some momentum, providing an outsider with a platform posed for more rapid change. In other situations, an outsider who shakes up the organization would be followed with an insider to channel and broaden the momentum. Also, an insider CMO could populate his or her team with outside talent and an outsider CMO could draw from inside the organization for team members thereby providing a group that would provide both outsider vitality and credibility and the insider organizational knowledge and relationships.

Enhancing Silo Marketing Talent

A strong marketing team is needed throughout the organization, not just in the central marketing group, for several reasons. First, a strong marketing presence in the silos will reduce the need to justify brand and marketing strategy. The conversation can be elevated. Second, whatever level of central control the CMO achieves, silo organizations will still have a design and implementation role that will require talent. Dow Corning has a global marketing excellence council that leads in building up the marketing capability of the firm. It detects capability gaps and develops initiatives to fill them through outside hiring, training initiatives, and mentoring programs. The council sponsored, for example, a "lunch and learn" program around lunch events. At GE, the CMO has a program of not only identifying potential marketing talent throughout the firm but also influencing their career paths.

Training Systems

Training and upgrading the marketing talent throughout the team is a key part of the equation. In general, they will need marketing skills in functional areas, the process models and information system, the brand and marketing strategy, and trends and issues around the markets in which the firm is engaged. Developing a training program starts with understanding the knowledge and skill gaps that result from an evaluation of the marketing talent. What should be the training priorities?

A basic tool is formal training programs that can be developed or accessed. Eli Lilly established the Lilly Marketing Institute, aimed at communicating the marketing planning framework so that everyone is speaking the same planning language. Unilever, recognizing that having its decentralized units go their own way was a liability, started in 1999 its global Unilever Marketing Academy.[5] One goal of its 150 courses and workshops is to get a common management system distributed throughout the world. A challenge for any training program is to gain participation—everyone is busy, and training is a choice. Unilever learned that it was helpful to focus on bringing the courses close to the issues that participants faced in their markets. Thus, when the budget for sponsorships went up, that topic was more prominent.

Starting a marketing curriculum in-house is not practical or useful for many firms that are not marketingcentric. A more effective and prudent course is to link to an established firmwide training program. The CMO at GE taps into the fabled GE training effort with its centerpiece John F. Welch Leadership Center at Crotonville, New York. With its $1 billion budget, it trains some six thousand employees each year and customers as well. The courses challenge and impact the firm—those for the top executives can result in strategy options and culture change that can be influential, even pathbreaking, for the firm. The goal of marketing is to introduce specialized marketing courses into this training system and to generate a marketing slant to the other programs that are directed to more general executive experiences.

If marketing training is undeveloped, it will be a challenge to get a budget and support to get it going. Here are some suggestions. First, access external well-developed training programs at major business schools. They have the advantage of being in place and offer the flexibility of dialing up the issues of the moment: digital marketing, for example. Second, for an in-house program, make sure that it focuses on priority-need areas and that it contains material that can be applied. Getting perceived value is the key to buying-in and participating. Third, for in-house programs, focus efforts on one or two types, such as brand strategy planning or touch point analysis. It is unrealistic to do too much. Fourth, consider online training since it will address schedule pressures felt by many.

While formal training surely has its place, there are a host of other ways to stimulate and pass on knowledge. IBM sponsors frequent speakers who access IBMers around the world with a combination of audio conferencing and intranet-based presentation material. Prophet has monthly "brand raps," where a brand strategy for a client is presented by conference meeting and passes on articles and books that are relevant.

New approaches and tools will be needed as the firm and the brand group and issues evolve. Honda upgrades its brand group with a monthly workshop with an executive from the Dentsu Brand Creation Group. The GE Crotonville center has a two-day "Industry 2015" series, such as Healthcare 2015 or Energy 2015, to stretch the minds of executives for whom these topics are central to their strategy.

Building a Cross-Silo Marketing Team

The central marketing group must engage the whole organization. A powerful device to achieve both involvement and buy-in is the use of cross-silo teams or councils of relevant managers, a subject for the next chapter.

Gaining traction for the CMO office, elevating marketing's role, and capturing synergy across silos is not easy, but it can be done and is being done by establishing credibility, gaining involvement, and delivering results.

For Discussion

1. Does the CMO team have credibility and buy-in throughout the organization? If not, what are the problems and solutions?

2. Does the CMO team as a group lack any of the needed ingredients: knowledge of marketing, branding, markets, products, and the organization?

3. Is the CEO on board? If not, what can the CMO do to change that fact?

4. What programs will generate visible early wins? What is the program with the first home run potential?

5. Evaluate the relationships between the CMO team and the silo marketing groups. How could they be improved?

6. Evaluate the CMO team. What are the gaps, the weaknesses? What are the strengths? What are the implications?

Chapter 3

Use Teams and Other Routes to Silo Linking

Direction is 90 percent casting.

—old Hollywood adage

The team changes every year, but each team member's three implicit questions for [the coach] remain the same. "Do you care about me? Can I trust you? Are you committed to the success of our team?"

—Lou Holtz, football coach

ONE OF THE MOST famous management dictums, "structure follows strategy," represented the conclusion of the business historian Alfred Chandler in his 1962 book in which he studied the evolution of the organizational structure of four dominant companies of the first half of the twentieth century: General Motors (GM), DuPont, Standard Oil of New Jersey, and Sears, Roebuck.[1]

Business strategy, for many firms, now involves creating cooperation, synergy, and resource allocation over silo business units. The challenge is to develop organizational structures that will help overcome the stultifying parochialism and power of these silo groups and enable that strategy to succeed. Organizational structures and processes need to be developed that will create silo linking, whereby people can enhance cross-silo information flow and develop and implement programs across silos.

A variety of organizational devices are available for firms to use to forward silo linking. They can use some or all of them, depending on the circumstances and the people available to implement them. Teams, the most important in terms of their potential effectiveness and widespread use, are discussed first. The chapter then turns to other devices, such as informal and formal networks, liaisons, integrators, centers of excellence, matrix organizations, and centralized marketing groups.

Cross-Silo Marketing Teams

The most commonly used silo buster is probably cross-silo teams, in part because of their flexibility, versatility, and power to span silos. Virtually all siloed firms use cross-silo teams. Google, for example, with a highly centralized marketing group, still has some forty teams that it uses to drive a host of objectives. The question is not whether to use teams but how extensively, for what objectives, and how to make them effective.

Cross-silo teams are not a new idea. Alfred Sloan—who, as CEO of GM, showed the business world nearly a century ago the power of decentralization when he created the most famous silo organization of the day—in fact advocated the concept of a cross-silo team to generate coordination among silos such as Chevrolet, Buick, and Cadillac.[2] He noted in reflecting on that period that the cross-silo teams were needed to make sure that synergy, economies of scale, and shared ideas were realized. It is even truer today.

A cross-silo team will by definition involve people from different silos in different competitive contexts. It can be and often is a virtual team, which means that at least some of its members will be in different locations and the meetings will not be face-to-face. The composition of the team, its objective, its operating style, and its leadership can vary widely, but it would involve people from different silos working on a visibly worthwhile problem or opportunity that spans silos.

A successful cross-silo team can provide a role model for the organization. Others will see that the power of teams and cross-silo cooperation can pay off. A series of team efforts will help the organization gain experience at how to create and manage effective teams and identify who are good team members and team leaders. Teams that generate visible success have the potential to help develop a collaboration culture in the organization. Unsuccessful teams, on the other hand, have the potential of solidifying silo walls and undercutting any collaboration culture effort.

Teams also create personal relationships and networks that are qualitatively different from casual interaction at meetings or social events and can stimulate or support cross-silo initiatives and communication way beyond the team scope. The use of teams is a way to cross-fertilize the organization and develop or support a coordination culture that could be exploited over time.

A team is often labeled as a council, as in Visa's global brand management council, which consists of the CMOs of the Visa regions and meets quarterly in person and more often by phone. The term *council* has more of a collaborative, strategic connotation, and it also implies more authority. HP has a customer experience council that systematically identifies drivers of customer problems at every touch point and develops enterprisewide solutions. The team is occasionally termed a board, as in IBM's global marketing board, consisting of the top marketing officers of the silo units. The term *board* has an even more authoritative ring to it than *council*.

Teams can tackle a wide variety of cross-silo issues. A team, for example, could influence the creation of cross-silo customer offerings that allow customer and product lines to be leveraged. Or it could manage a silo-spanning brand. Or it could manage a brand portfolio controlling the entry of new brands and the consolidation of existing brands. Or it could develop and guide a cross-silo brand and marketing effectiveness measurement system. Or it could allocate marketing expenditures. Still another use is to coordinate the support of a major sponsorship. The experiences of ChevronTexaco, Pharmacia, Unilever, Dow Corning, and P&G illustrate this.

ChevronTexaco developed a global brand council that included top-level operating people representing the major geographies, products, and businesses of the firm. The council was charged to sponsor a process that would lead to a coherent brand portfolio, an effective brand identity for the top organizational brands, and a management system that would allow all brands to be actively managed. The challenge was to create a new structure and process in a mature organization with a group sourced from all over the world. Because its members were senior operating people, the council was in a position to make decisions and see them implemented. Further, its recommendations about the corporate brand had credibility because few parts of the organization were uninformed and not represented.

The ChevronTexaco global brand council developed another charge after the firm established the brand strategy process. It served to resolve conflicts between silo units, such as when brands, offerings, or marketing programs would overlap. It also provides a forum to identify issues going forward, such as the advisability of a major sponsorship. The council would form working teams to address such issues as needed.

Pharmacia developed a global team to manage its business. The core management units included four regional vice presidents for North America, Europe, Asia/Pacific, and Latin America. Each had profit and loss (P&L) responsibility and managed the country business units that also had P&L responsibility. The four regional vice presidents meet regularly to coordinate marketing globally, especially if a new product is to be planned and launched. The goal was to pool the expertise of the global team.

At Unilever, each of the forty global brands is managed by a global brand director who heads up a global brand team, which includes regional brand leaders. The role of the global brand team is to create more coherent management of the global brand through a closer working relationship between global and silo brand management. One task is to manage the brand equity and innovation stream. Another is to develop an agreed-on brand identity and plan the migration to that identity. A third is to develop and implement growth plans.

Those organizations that use teams usually develop a set of them to address different issues. Dow Corning, for example, has a team of teams. The commercial council determines the overall brand direction and drives the strategy to change the organization to deliver on the brand promise, which could include recommending new offerings and changes in metrics and performance measures. The brand council, which includes the CMO and a marketing representative of each division, approves new brands added to the portfolio and manages how master brands are to be adapted to divisions. The integrated communication team, consisting of the corporate communication manager plus the communication managers from the silo divisions, guides communication programs horizontally (across industries and within products) and vertically (within an industry across products). The global marketing excellence council leads in building up the marketing capability of the firm by identifying capability gaps and the need for new talent or training initiatives.

P&G's core organizational device is the management teams for its twenty-two product categories that collectively include some three hundred brands, over forty of which have sales exceeding $500 million. The category manager teams manage the business over brands, over countries and regions, and over functional areas including R&D and manufacturing. In addition, P&G marketing manages two internal teams that deal with category silos. The first—the fifteen-person global marketing officer's leadership team, representing groupings of categories and the regions—sets priorities, considers opportunities that cross silo boundaries, develops initiatives (such as leveraging retail data and knowledge), and manages career paths of key executives. The forty-person brand building capability council has representatives from categories and regions plus people from outside marketing, such as design and external communications. This team focuses on driving adoption of capabilities such as targeting, equity management, and brand portfolio strategy.

With numerous teams, there can be overlapping issues or tasks, and it can be a challenge to communicate and coordinate between teams. One approach is to have some people span teams. The marketing research manager, for example, could participate in all the brand teams and provide the link between them. Another approach is to have a "super" or coordinating team consisting of the leaders of related teams.

Task Force Teams

Teams or councils usually refer to permanent groups that have an ongoing responsibility for an area. If a group is assigned a task that has a defined time frame, it is often termed a task force team or task force rather than a team. For example, a task force team might be used to create a brand identity and brand portfolio strategy for an organization. Their output might be handed off to a permanent team that would implement the strategy and manage it over time. The management of a defined sponsorship over silos could be managed by a task force.

MasterCard, for example, created a series of task force teams to manage one of its major sponsorships, the soccer World Cup. MasterCard started its World Cup sponsorship in 1994 as a way to become a world player and to combat Visa with its "Everywhere you want to be" position and Olympic sponsorship. The global effort involved a World Cup advertising campaign featuring the iconic Pelé, newsletters, promotion execution guides, sponsorship manuals, a promotion video, Pelé photos, corporate hospitality invitations, and welcome kits. Regions outside the United States followed its lead in sponsoring regional events and national teams.

Leveraging the sponsorship globally and encouraging the MasterCard bank affiliates throughout the world to participant was an organizational challenge in part because of the differences in cultures and abilities to implement a sponsorship program. The effort started with the assignment of a U.S. promotions executive to Europe to play a liaison role for those who were not experienced with event sponsorship. Later, MasterCard formed the global World Cup product team. Consisting of a member from each region, it met quarterly to transfer knowledge, expertise, and best practices for leveraging the sponsorship.

A task force team can help to jumpstart cross-silo communication. At Carlsberg, the heads of nine European markets formed a group that was first tasked with identifying a set of best-practice dimensions such as segmentation, pricing, sales, advertising, and so on. They were then asked to assess their performance on each dimension. The process was not only stimulating but led to real change. In consumer segmentation, every country used different schemes—from age to needs to lifestyle. Within three months, the nine coalesced around a common scheme.[3]

Keys to Successful Teams

A team experience can result in both dramatic success and implosions that can set back collaboration for years. The good news is that there is a significant body of research about what makes teams effective, and the resulting guidelines can help those that don't insist on a hurried team implementation and a do-it-yourself attitude. Many of the findings are particularly relevant to teams spanning silos. Figure 3-1 suggests four dimensions of team management.

Clarity of Mission

The team needs clarity of mission. In a classic study of team effectiveness involving an appraisal of some fifty teams from thirty companies,

FIGURE 3-1

Keys to successful teams

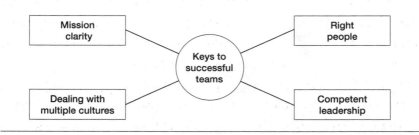

IMC—Integrated Marketing Communication

In 1972, a Y&R CEO, Ed Ney, announced that the firm would create a team of specialists representing different modalities, such as advertising, direct response, PR, design, and promotion, in order to provide a combined team approach to a client's communication needs. The effort, supported by acquiring firms, was labeled "the whole egg" and was implemented in part by an acquisition strategy. For the last thirty-five years, Y&R and other advertising firms and communication conglomerates such as WPP, Interpublic, and Publicis have attempted to deliver the whole egg. They have had, on average, a remarkable lack of success, particularly long-term success.

A basic limitation of the IMC team is that the vitality of periodically having an open competition for ideas is missing. With independent communication partners for advertising, promotion, and so on, if the communication programs get stagnant or ineffective, a group of competing firms can be asked to submit their best ideas. The winner becomes the new partner. When a commitment is made to an IMC team, the client is reluctant to disrupt the team in part because of relationship issues but also because the whole point of the IMC team is to create continuity over time as well as over modalities.

Three other problems apply to both internal and external communication silos. One is that these silos regard themselves as competitors for resources, each believing that its approach is the most effective. Another is that modalities simply do not communicate well, in part because they do not conceptualize the marketplace in the same way and in part because they have very different performance measures. A third problem is that the leaders who could provide a strategic, integrating vision are in short supply.

Recently, the need for IMC has become intense. Reliance on mass media as the cornerstone of the communication program is fading. In its place is an array of tools that are much more important than ever before, such as sponsorship, PR, digital marketing, social marketing, event marketing, media buying, and more. The concept of "media neutral" integrated communication has become more valued and, for many, critical. The reality of global strategies provides still another motivating impetus. In that context, there has been a flurry of new team-based initiatives toward IMC.

Communication companies are renewing their efforts. McCann Erickson Worldwide has combined an agency network that includes an advertising firm and firms representing digital customer management, public relations, brand consulting and design, events, promotions, and sponsorship.[4] A core framework called the demand chain serves to provide a common platform and language across disciplines. McCann Erickson searches for a strategy and big idea that will work across vehicles. Fifteen of its twenty biggest accounts use five of the firms. WPP is another firm that has aggressively put together teams. WPP created a new firm called Da Vinci to handle the global communication needs of Dell Computer; the staff was drawn from the cadre of some 250 communication firms under the WPP umbrella.

Client firms are also moving toward creative organizational forms to deliver IMC. P&G has adopted an IMC team for several brands. It starts by identifying the most important modality for that brand. For Pampers, for example, it could be the Web site and social marketing because the driver is the concept of baby care. For another brand, it could be sponsorship. But the principal modality does not have to be advertising. The best agency in the modality for P&G is then selected and the team coleaders are selected from that agency and from P&G. These coleaders will then assemble a group of supporting agencies from which a team will be formed. The leadership will direct and coordinate the team. A key element is that the team will be compensated as a team—the leaders can apportion the budget as they see fit. Another is that the agencies involved do not have to be affiliated. Rather, they have to be the best and willing to give P&G their "A team" effort. The result is a far cry from the disjointed set of firms and people that is normally involved in a brand.

What have we learned from the many efforts to create cross-silo IMC teams? A lot, actually. We know that the task is difficult. It is difficult to get started, and it is really difficult to keep going. Even successful efforts last for years and then fade or spin out of control when one or more of the critical enabling factors weaken or become absent. We also know that the chances of success are higher when there is a:

- **CEO mandate with a compelling business rationale for IMC.** CEO support makes the silo barriers shrink.

- **Strong brand strategy driving the effort.** The strategy must be the integrator, and it must be clear and compelling. Google guides with a set of ten values that guide all brand building, such as to focus on the user (clean, simple interfaces), do one thing really well, and be fast.

- **Great idea from one of the modalities.** Chapter 7 elaborates.

- **Client-led effort.** The clout and strategic sense from the client helps keep the external silos on the same page.

- **Strong strategic leader.** The leaders should have organizational influence, a strategic perspective, and team leadership skills. At Apple, one of the few firms that have excelled at IMC, Steve Jobs plays that role.

- **Compensation system that is team based.** Often, that is a radical departure from the norm of many of the participants and is not easy to implement.

- **Team drawn from a single firm.** This has worked relatively well for firms such as Dentsu, McCann-Erickson Worldwide and Y&R. It has been less successful when the participants share a common holding company, such as WPP or Publicis, and even less so when the firms are independent, although even in this last condition, an IMC teaming model with a strong client leader such as P&G can still work.

McKinsey strategists Jon R. Katzenbach and Douglas K. Smith highlight the role of common purpose and performance goals in their definition of a team: "A team is a small number of people with complementary skills who are committed to a common purpose, set of performance goals, and approach for which they hold themselves mutually accountable."[5]

The CMO must clearly identify a mission and establish the problem or opportunity for which the team's work will be a solution. The case must credibly demonstrate that there will be a payoff for the silos that will merit investment in time and resources. If the charge comes from top executives, it is likely to be more persuasive, especially if the importance of the task is related to the strategy of the firm. It is even better if the charge has an element of inspiration and promise that the progress will be monitored by the executive team or someone with stature in the firm. The clarity and value of the mission will affect the ability of the team to recruit members and be effective in reaching goals.

The team will almost always benefit from taking time to discuss and refine the mission. As Katzenbach and Smith said, "The best teams invest a tremendous amount of time and effort exploring, shaping, and agreeing on a purpose that belongs to them both collectively and individually. This 'purposing' activity continues through the life of the team."[6] P&G, with a lot of experience in cross-silo teams, engages in the "relentless pursuit of clarity" so that there is no ambiguity about the task. When a member is asked why the team exists, there should not be an awkward pause—an answer should be at the ready.

The mission should be translated into performance goals. If, for example, the mission is to create a brand vision and adapt it to every silo, the goals could include getting input from key participants, creating a master brand vision, conducting adaptation sessions, and creating internal communication programs.

Performance goals provide several functions. First, they clarify the mission itself because specific goals tend to make the abstract more tangible and less ambiguous. Second, they help focus the team effort and make it easier to avoid being diverted. Third, they provide the existence of wins along the way that can help morale, create energy, and even attract resources. They also can generate the fear of failure, which can also be a great motivator. Finally, they can be the basis for the evaluation of the team.

The Right People

The success of the cross-silo marketing team starts with the quality and type of team participants. When the CMO forms a team by automatically picking a set of people who have the seemingly appropriate organizational title, there is a risk that the resulting team will lack some necessary ingredient or that the team chemistry will be faulty. Beware also the well-credentialed person who lacks respect and a track record but is available for a new "committee" assignment. The available people are not always the most suitable. Team members should have some or all of the needed characteristics, such as silo expertise, functional expertise, interpersonal skills, and change agent characteristics.

If the job is to coordinate across silos, the team should include people with silo expertise. They will bring to the table knowledge of not only the silo's business and market, but also the relevant organizational realities that exist. Often, however, there may be too many silos to be represented—a team cannot accommodate each of one hundred country silos, for example. Then the silo representation issue can become delicate because people will be needed who can represent and communicate across a group of silos.

Functional expertise relates to the job at hand. If there is to be a coordination of the brand vision, the team should include people with knowledge of brands and brand equity. If it is a sponsorship-oriented team, it should include those with experience in running and coordinating silo efforts toward a sponsor.

Interpersonal skills can be underrated. The essence of a team is the ability to thrive in an open give-and-take atmosphere. Characteristics such as being able to listen well, articulate ideas, live with some constructive conflict, and accept group-oriented objectives are important attributes of team members. These are particularly important in cross-silo contexts where the objectives of the silos may not be aligned. The people on the team must be collaborators who will work with others and will commit time to the effort. Even one disinterested or negative person can disrupt the group effort. Tom Kelley, the innovation guru, talks about the destructive power of the group member who takes pride in inserting "let me just play the devil's advocate for a minute . . ."[7] Realism is good but persistent negativity is not.

However talented the people, working collaboratively in general and making groups work more effectively are skills that can be enhanced. Some firms, such as Seagate Technology (see "The Ultimate Builder") have developed and implemented training programs to improve those skills. The training programs not only provide skill improvement but also help create or enhance a culture of working together. Research has found that ongoing training on group effectiveness can make a real difference. The problem, of course, is making the case that the added time and commitment are feasible and worthwhile.

When the task includes installing a program that involves change in a silo organization, the silo team members must be change agents. That can mean that they should be at a high enough level to have authority to implement. However, the best change agents will often have more than authority; they might have a personal ability to instigate change perhaps by persuasion or by tapping into the culture of the silo group, and have ready access to the necessary skills, resources, and authority within their silos. The CEO of Intel once said that all teams should have a wild duck, someone who is willing to stir things up.

Competent Leadership

Running a team, particularly one that is addressing cross-silo problems, can be challenging. A gifted leader can make a difference, for sure. The CMO of Syrutra, the Chinese dairy firm, believes that the differentiating quality of successful teams is the quality of leadership. He believes that effective leaders need to be both good communicators and delegators: the team has to know their purpose and the members their role; and the team needs to be given the freedom to develop and own proposals and initiatives. Other observers of team performance have suggested that organizational stature and substantive knowledge and skills are qualities to look for in picking team leaders.

The Ultimate Team Builder

Since 2000, Bill Watkins, the CEO of Seagate Technology, has hosted the ultimate team-building experience—Eco Seagate. Each year, two hundred Seagate employees (selected from over two thousand applicants) gather in New Zealand's South Island for a weeklong team-building experience. The participants are divided into five-person teams that are artfully formed to provide the right mix of people. The teams engage in a host of activities designed to challenge people's assumptions about life, job, and teaming—activities such as yoga, tai chi, tae kwon do, a Maori dance, and orienteering, plus meetings addressing topics such as fear of commitment and avoiding accountability. The capstone is a 40K team adventure race involving climbing a glacier, mountain biking, kayaking, and riding a cable over a gorge. Finishing is all about the team—trust, commitment, and cooperation.

The motivation for Eco Seagate is to help build a more collaborative, team-oriented company. Watkins observed that in a company's start-up phase there is a natural camaraderie and team spirit that fades as the company gets large and silos form. He wanted to bring the team spirit to the large organization. Eco Seagate is the vehicle—it takes a team experience to a whole new level.

Source: Jeffrey M. O'Brien, "Team Building in Paradise," *Fortune*, May 26, 2008, 113–120.

Leading a team involves a host of decisions and activities. Fortunately, the experience of managing teams has been studied extensively and the resulting literature on team management provides some practical guidelines for team leaders:

- Draw on the team mission and performance goals to create commitment, enthusiasm, and group accountability.

- Handle conflict openly—get it on the table, and find a way to resolve it or live with it. Do not let offline conversations and e-mails undercut the team's performance.

- Delegate. Let the team members take ownership of aspects of the team charge. Doing so will get them involved and leverage what they bring to the table.

- Involve those outside the team, whether in interviews or task forces, in order to have more direct and indirect support for implementation of the ultimate team findings.

- Make sure that there is a process, a meeting rhythm, a schedule that will work for the team and its members. Spend whatever time is necessary to get that in place.

- Develop communication and information-sharing rules and norms so that the process is open and inclusive.

- Start with discipline around the team's mission, but over time be prepared to relax that discipline as the project evolves and the team gets more confidence and competence to advance the ball.

Dealing with Multiple Cultures

A cross-silo team will often have very different cultures. A culture is reflected in norms of behavior, values, perceptions, and attitudes. Mixing cultures can be a positive element leading to creative ideas. One of the points of cross-silo activity is to enhance creativity by providing a wide dispersion of ideas.

One source of culture difference is that a marketing person may have a different way of looking at things and communicating than someone from engineering or R&D. And within marketing, someone from sales might have a very different perspective from advertising or branding. At Syrutra, one of the biggest team challenges was to integrate and involve the team member representing sales into marketing teams. The goal is to blend the tactical, executional orientation of sales with the strategic orientation of the marketing team members to gain a healthy balance of strategy and execution. Engaging the sales persons and getting everyone to broaden their perspectives is an ongoing challenge.

A concern facing global firms is the difference between country cultures. A variety of dimensions of culture associated with regions or groups of countries can have a marked effect on cross-county team activity.[8] The pioneering work in this area was done in the 1970s by Geert Hofstede, who postulated several sharp differences, including long-term versus short-term, masculinity versus femininity, uncertainty avoidance, power distance, and individualism versus collectivism.[9] The latter two are particularly relevant.

Power distance refers to the degree of vertical inequality among people in the organization. In high–power distance countries such as China, Japan, Brazil, Venezuela, India, France, Hong Kong, Mexico, and the Arab countries, there is a tendency to avoid challenging those organizationally superior and even to defer to them in contributing. In one "free flowing" discussion of brand issues with a fifteen-person Japanese brand team that I experienced, virtually the only spokesperson was the CMO, even though others were asked for opinions—a not uncommon circumstance in Japan. When teams include participants from high-power countries, the CMO should seek ways to increase the contribution of those with cultural inhibitions. For example, they might have a specific assignment including a presentation so that their contribution does not rely on volunteering.

Individualism versus collectivism defines the difference between collectivist cultures, where there a tendency to seek consensus, to rely on groups, and to be uncomfortable standing out as an individual; and individualistic cultures, where independent thinking and action are accepted and even fostered. Countries in Asia and South America tend to have collectivist cultures, while North American and European countries tend to have individualistic cultures. When these two culture types are mixed, a concern of the team should be that the participants from a collectivist culture will defer to the group and the participants from an individualist culture will dominate.

A team and its leader must be sensitive to these cross-culture realities because they can influence the interpretation of communication and the willingness and ability to participate. The way the team is composed and the way meetings are run can ameliorate the effect and turn diversity into the asset that it should be.

Virtual Teams

Cross-silo teams often must be *virtual teams*—teams that involve people in different locations. With audio conferencing, e-mailing, instant messaging, and shared document capability so well developed and reliable, it can be feasible, even easy, to hold meetings and to develop communication systems that tie a dispersed group together and enable joint work. As a practical matter, videoconferencing, with its technical limitations, has not been considered essential for many organizations except as part of a get-to-know-you phase because audio conferencing is so flexible. A member can be in an airport lounge or in a hotel and still tap into an audio conference. However, the world of videoconferencing is changing.

New technology, termed *telepresence*, which aims to make participants feel as if they are present, is promising to change practices. Several firms such as Google and Cisco now use the new telepresence technology extensively. With cameras on personal computers and in virtually every conference room, it becomes feasible to have pictures of all the participants on a screen along with a PowerPoint presentation. Seeing facial and body language can enhance communication and affect relationships. By 2008 Cisco had conducted some 100,000 telepresence meetings, of which 16,000 saved some $70 million in travel expenses.[10]

Several obvious forces drive the use of virtual units. Teams that span countries or span product silos in different locations would find meeting regularly face-to-face extremely expensive and, usually, just not feasible. The fact is that members of task forces and teams have other jobs and demands on their schedules and are often members of multiple teams. Introducing travel time into an already difficult schedule would make the difficult become impossible. As a result, the ability of the group to meet would be compromised, as would its effectiveness.

Further, the motivating problems or tasks often are attached with some urgency. The virtual format enables firms to move quickly. Suppose a large global firm has decided to review its communications program. A communications company such as WPP could in a matter of days create a virtual team—involving people from its family of firms that represent market research, public relations, advertising, sponsorships, and regions such as Asia and Europe—that could quickly marshal an impressive breadth of information, insights, and skills. Getting the team together requires only finding a hole of a few hours in the team members' schedules. The team's subsequent activities can be coordinated by e-mail and intranet-based sharing of information and documents, in addition to meetings. Virtual teams have in many cases an indispensable role in addressing silo-spanning issues. However, they create their own set of problems and can too easily dissolve into ineffectiveness or, worse, accentuate instead of reduce the silo culture. A person hearing an audio conference comment or reading an e-mail can too easily misinterpret its content or intent especially when different cultures are involved. In a virtual world, it is not possible to drop into an office and ask how a task or project is coming or why someone missed a meeting.

Succeeding with Virtual Teams

Succeeding in a virtual world requires some imagination and effort. Some of the keys to success in a nonvirtual world must become even more important. Further, there are new success guidelines that do not exist in the nonvirtual world. Drawing in part from a study of some fifty-five successful virtual task forces and teams, we can generate some suggestions:[11]

- Develop norms about how information is communicated, reflecting the fact that the flow of insights and information is particularly critical in virtual space. Such norms include how often to check the intranet site, what to post, how to comment, what information can be shared, having people say their name before speaking in audio conferencing, and calling out slide numbers during presentations.

- Develop a profile of the expertise and personal background interests of each member along with a picture so that the group can get to know each other. Start some meetings with an informal catch-up segment on people's personal lives. One firm introduces new members with two truths and a lie. The new members list three events from their past, and the challenge is to identify the lie.

- Manage the meetings well. Have background readings, agendas, and posting of working documents. Check in during meetings by, for example, asking members to vote on whether a certain issue was resolved. Create lists of action items, and identify the people who own those items.

- Provide training for members in group activities and the use of the supporting technology, since virtual groups may be particularly vulnerable to inadequate skills in group processes. The goal should be to make sure that unsatisfactory participation is not due to a lack of knowledge about or capability in group activities.

- Make sure that the efforts of the group and its members are visible by creating vehicles to communicate their efforts—for example, status reports to senior management and, in particular, to those the group members report to.

- Encourage ongoing discussion among group members. One firm pairs people and tasks them to interact. Another creates subgroup units that interact while addressing assigned tasks.

- Encourage participation in meetings while being sensitive to cultural and language inhibitions. Make sure that remote attendees stay involved and participate. Instead of asking for questions, ask specific people who are remote to identity concerns or issues.

- Reward the group participants by recognizing individual contributions and group accomplishments.

- Have a regular get-together to help the team evaluate the process, team development, the mission and progress toward it, and the behavior norms.

- Be concerned about work/life balance with global teams. It can be wearing to be on call at all hours.

Routes to Linking Silos

Teams or councils are not the only organizational devices to support cross-silo cooperation, as suggested by figure 3-2. Informal or formal networks, like teams, use cross-silo groups. The central marketing group can play a variety of coordination roles, such as liaison, integrator, or center of excellence entities. Finally, there are alternative organizational structures, such as the matrix or centralized marketing. It should be clear that it is not necessary to select one of these organizational forms; several could be employed.

Informal Networks

The most primitive and nonthreatening form of strategic linking is informal networks. An informal network based on personal relationships can be very powerful especially if supported by the right culture and reward system. At Monsanto, a person's networking capability is valued, and it becomes part of the performance evaluation. At Clorox, people are rotated between product silos in part to provide them with an expanded network of contacts. The CMO group can encourage informal networks by actions such as providing e-mail contact information to attendees at events or publicizing a best-practice author.

Informal networks, perhaps supported by a community Web site and an information coordinator, can be formed based on mutual interests or

FIGURE 3-2

Routes to linking silos

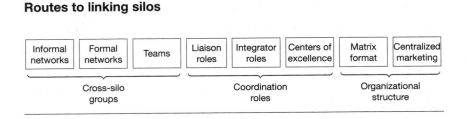

problems. Nestlé is an example of a firm that has developed informal networks around global customers. A country marketing team with a major customer such as Tesco or Wal-Mart will have motivation to keep in contact with counterparts in other countries to learn of intelligence about the customer's strategies and programs that work in their stores. HP has communities of interest that meet monthly for a one-hour audio conference to discuss a topic of interest.

Informal networks, although potentially influential, are ad hoc, difficult to manage, and vulnerable to the presence and motivation of a few key people. Because there is self-selection, the right set of people are rarely included and motivated to participate. Boundaries are hard to define, and information overload often emerges, with the percentage of useful information drifting down, followed by reduced participation and effectiveness. The big opportunity for the CMO team is formal networks.

Formal Networks

Firms can enhance and manage silo-spanning communication with a formal network that is characterized by having an enhanced level of direction, formal leadership, and defined membership. Less is left to the vagaries of the interests and motivations of a random group of people. A formal network can be organized around a variety of themes, such as customer groups, market trends, customer experience contexts, geographies, or functional areas such as sponsorship or digital marketing. The groups should be relevant to ongoing issues and problems, and the information actionable so that people are motivated to participate.

A CMO can play a host of management roles, including creating the network and setting its objectives. The CMO can assign or recruit the target people, which might include a core group who would be relevant because of their position or knowledge set. In general, the group should contain people with different backgrounds and perspectives because the power of the network will come from marshaling diversity. The objectives should be clear and measurable and include participation measures as well as substantive network goals because participation is a key success factor for any network.

Another potential CMO role is to create network leadership and infrastructure. A network leader not only must be content credible, but also needs skills in getting people involved. The CMO team can also develop the supporting infrastructure, such as internal blogs, community Web sites, or a place in the firm's "knowledge hub," which is described in the next chapter.

One challenge facing the formal network is to get participation. Incentives such as recognition for contributions or rewards such as off-site meetings perceived as fun and worthwhile can help. The lack of participation can occur in part because of participants' not knowing that something relevant has surfaced in the network. The publication of visible and interesting outputs can spark a person to check out the current network output. Managing information overload can also affect participation. If it takes too much time to process too much information people will lose interest. The use of information summary mechanisms that filter and condense the information can be one role of a network leader or network facilitator.

A major energy company used a set of best-practice networks, which consisted of people around the world from the firm and partner organizations who had expertise and interest in certain areas, such as the introduction of new products, brand architecture, or retail site presentation. Each network had a senior management sponsor who provided support and direction and a leader/facilitator who provided the necessary energy, thought leadership, and continuity. Relevant insights and best practices were then sought out and posted on an easy-to-access intranet site managed by the network group.

Liaison Roles

A central marketing group can assign a person as a liaison with one or more of the silo groups, perhaps country or region or product silos. That person would be expected to be knowledgeable about the silo group's issues and needs and make sure that the silo group was aware of the central marketing resources. Or there could be a liaison in the silo unit with the job of linking that unit to the central marketing group to facilitate the silo unit's ability to access the resources and programs of the central marketing group. A liaison will serve as a source of both information and expertise to both the silo and the central marketing group. Being on the ground makes the linking effort more effective.

The location of the liaison can have both practical and symbolic implications. The silo group's liaison could be located in the central marketing group, or the central marketing group's liaisons could be dispersed in order to get them closer to the operating managers. For example, a major global financial services firm has a marketing team that includes several "account executives" for operating units such as investment banking and wealth management who are located wherever the business center of gravity is for that unit. Toyota has home office people in the country silos who play liaison roles although their charge is much broader.

The introduction of liaison roles provides more structure and positive management than does the reliance on networks. It also generates little stress on the organization, assuming that those in the liaison role are knowledgeable and well suited to a collaborative mission. However, the ability of a liaison to resolve conflicts and precipitate action will be limited.

Integrator Roles

An integrator role sets up someone who is accountable for coordinated programs. So there could be an integrator charged with sponsorship efforts across countries, for example. He or she would make sure that the silo units know about the silo options for supporting and leveraging a sponsorship and that their input is heard. The challenge would then be to get the major firm sponsorship fully leveraged across the silo units.

An important integrator role is that of a brand manager for a master brand that spans products or countries. Filling a role similar to the classic brand manager role but more strategic in scope, he or she would provide guidance and leadership for the brand, its vision, how that vision should be adapted to the silo contexts, and the development of synergistic brand-building programs.

The integrator, even with little direct authority, may still have a significant ability to influence actions and achieve objectives that span silos. A key is to have a person who has credibility with respect to relevant expertise, has visibility into top management, and has exceptional communication, interpersonal, and conflict resolution skills.

Centers of Excellence

A center of excellence within a central marketing team, introduced in an earlier chapter, will have a group that focuses on a particular issue that spans silos, such as a customer trend, an emerging product subcategory, or a technology. The center could be staffed by a single person or a small group. The charge would be to gain deep insights into the issue and to stay abreast of developments. The center should actively reach out to the silo teams in order to both receive and disperse information and thus provide a catalyst for communication and information flow.

Nestlé USA has several centers of excellence, including one for moms and kids and another on the Hispanic market. In each case, the centers formed an advisory council with members from the silos for which the topic would be relevant. The council provides silo-based information and participates in insight meetings. Nestlé headquarters has a larger center of excellence for health and wellness, a Nestlé corporate priority. Clorox has centers of excellence for functional areas such as advertising, sponsorship, and Web site development that support the service supplier role of the CMO team. Prophet has centers of excellence for marketing effectiveness and innovation to support two expansions of its consulting capability.

Matrix Organizations

A CMO has the most influence over someone who reports to him or her and the least over someone who reports to another. The reporting relationship determines who does the direction and evaluation. Switching the reporting structure can make a huge difference in symbolic as well as practical ways.

The matrix structure, illustrated in figure 3-3, has the silo marketing team reporting to the central marketing group as well as to the silo general managers. It allows a person to have two homes, two bosses, and two sets of objectives. The silo people may still spend 90 percent of their

FIGURE 3-3

Organizational structures

Silo structure	Matrix structure	Centralized marketing

time with the silo teams, but the objectives of the central marketing group will be visible and meaningful to them. Matrix structures are common in global corporations where the marketing units of geographic silos are crossed with marketing in product divisions.

Having the silo marketing team report to the CMO as well as to the silo management provides a way for the CMO to gain influence in a silo marketing effort. This link could be a "dotted" line, which means that it is a secondary reporting link, as opposed to a "solid" line. The relationship could tilt the other way, of course. The solid line could be to the CMO, and the dotted line could be to the silo executive. In some contexts, the dotted versus solid line decision can make a big difference. The CMO at Seagram's found that the regional marketing heads were much more attuned to connect when there was a solid line reporting arrangement. In any case, the CMO will exert more control and oversight with a dotted line link than if there were no reporting relationship at all. Monsanto has a primary manager for every marketing staff member but also sometimes has three or four dotted-line relationships. Each of these contributes to the evaluation process, often in the context of a meeting of senior executives.

At GE, the matrix organization has a significant impact on personnel decisions. The CMO carries out performance reviews annually, for the marketing staff in the business units with whom the CMO has a dotted line relationship. For each of these staffers, the CMO identifies skill gaps, needs for training, and those people who should be promoted or moved to other contexts to advance their career path. The goal is to generally upgrade the marketing team throughout the firm.

The problem is that the matrix structure can be unstable. There will be tension between the objectives and personalities that are involved in the two reporting relationships. Adjustments to change can be stressful. The demands on the HR and IT support functions can be challenging. The matrix organization tends to work best when it is an interim solution or when one of the relationships is a dotted line and the priorities are therefore more transparent.

Centralized Marketing

The ultimate solution is to centralize marketing. When a new CMO came into Allstate in the early 2000s, an early move was to make the several hundred marketing people residing in product silos report to him. The result was support for a very dramatic change in the way that marketing strategy and tactics were pursued at Allstate.

Dell Services decided that the problems of developing nonredundant competences in marketing and being able to deliver systems solutions were not adequately addressed with collaborative teams, and it decided to centralize marketing across all silos. The first step was to use an integrator role for eighteen months. Progress was made, but to go to the next level, the new CEO, brought in by Michael Dell to centralize the business, decided to centralize marketing, which meant that all marketing people reported to the CMO of Dell Services. Some of the people formerly in silo units were assigned to have as a second job that of a liaison to the silo group but were now on the CMO's staff. A few silo marketing people could not adjust to the new context, which meant for them a smaller, more specialized aperture, and they had to leave the organization. In addition, the innovation, part of the DNA of the autonomous silos, needed to be nurtured in the new context.

An organization can engage in minicentralization by reducing the number of silos, which will reduce the number of marketing teams, thereby strengthening each and enhancing resource allocation. Clorox, for example, reduced the number of divisions, which acted as highly autonomous silos, from five to three. GM has consolidated its eight car divisions into four: Chevrolet, Saturn, premium (Cadillac, Saab, and Hummer), and Buick/Pontiac/GMC.

In at least the most visible cases in which the organization has successfully centralized marketing, there has been a strong strategic vision to justify the decision, a change agent from outside the firm, a sense of crisis or at least a serious and growing problem, and the visible leadership in this direction from the CEO.

Which Routes?

What routes should a firm employ? The answer will depend on the context, but directionally most firms would benefit from a move toward more influence by the CMO team. Among the considerations are the following:

- What role is the CMO team playing? Their role will affect the use of organizational options. If it is a strategic captain or strategic partnership role, then the firm might consider the use of a matrix or a centralized organization. The other options could be in play whatever role the CMO assumes.

- How significant is the opportunity represented by enhanced silo linking? How serious is the problem or crisis for which silo linking is part of the solution?

- How isolated are the silos? And what degree of interdependence does the task at hand require? If the silo barriers are high and the need for strategic linking is high, then a more aggressive organizational structure might be appropriate.

- What people are available to implement the options? It takes motivated, competent people to staff any of these options except perhaps the informal network. Even when the right people are present, their time is usually precious because the opportunity cost can be high. They are likely to be the same people who are filling key strategic and tactical roles for the organization.

- What are the risks associated with failure? An effort to engage in silo linking that is ineffective or, worse, flames out can set back the achievement of strategic linking objectives for years or even decades. A failure or disappointment can taint all efforts that follow.

Creating a Cross-Silo Culture

The use of cross-silo organizational devices can help break down the silo barriers. But the real payoff comes from creating culture and reward systems that support the collaboration across silos. The goal should be to create an organizational norm to work together to address problems and opportunities.

A pivotal issue is the reward structure. When the dominant role of incentives is to reward silo behavior and performance, it is not surprising that teams and other strategic linking devices struggle. The key to success is to adjust incentives to encourage cross-silo activities. At the individual level, that means explicitly measuring and rewarding collaborative behavior. At the firm level, that means creating incentives to look beyond silo success to cross-silo initiatives and firm performance indicators.

For Discussion

1. What cross-silo teams are now operating? What is the mission of each? Evaluate their performance.

2. What are the major cross-silo problems or missed opportunities? Could additional teams be used to address them?

3. What are the keys to team success in your organization?

4. What other strategic linking devices are being used? Evaluate their effectiveness. Should others be employed?

Chapter 4

Develop a Common Planning Process and Information System

Plans are nothing, planning is everything.

—Dwight Eisenhower

Things should be made as simple as possible, but not simpler.

—Albert Einstein

APPARENTLY sophisticated marketing firms often lack a common planning process across their silo units. In too many cases, the silo units are able to use their homegrown planning process, and the results are predictably uneven and ad hoc. Even when a common planning process exists, it is often too open to interpretation and adaptation or is so convoluted, full of jargon, and confusing that it is ineffective or worse. There is often a lot of potential improvement available in the silo planning and strategy creation arenas. And it is a rare information system that is effective and widely used.

A standardized brand and/or marketing program, one that is virtually the same across country or product silos, is rarely optimal. What is optimal is to have both a planning process, including templates and frameworks, and a supporting information system that are the same everywhere. Firms that lack such assets have a hard time generating cross-silo communication, to say nothing of synergistic strategies and programs. A key part of the facilitator role is to work toward that objective by introducing and supporting processes and systems that will be common across silos.

Having a common planning process yields two payoffs. The first is to provide the basis for communication by creating common vocabulary, measures, information, and decision structures. Such commonality in the context of planning is by itself a potentially powerful stimulus to not only communication but also the creation of synergistic marketing programs and offerings. Two silo managers, simply by discussing a trend analysis affecting both, can stimulate strategy options with potential synergy. If each had a problem with one of the measurement metrics, a basis for problem sharing and problem solving would exist. If both report segmentation strategies in the context of a marketing plan, a comparison might be instructive.

A second payoff is to enable the organization to develop a minimal level of professionalism throughout the silo units. Unless there is a clear, accepted planning process with understandable and actionable components, every unit will go its own way, and, inevitably, some will as a result be mismanaged strategically and will find it difficult to convert strategy into tactical programs. Executives will find it difficult to help underperforming silos that develop strategies according to their own planning process. Management training without a common planning process will be ineffective or, more likely, just will not happen.

Figure 4-1 shows six components of the silo planning process. Three—market/self-analysis, silo business strategy, and silo market strength—are part of a silo strategic analysis. The silo marketing strategy consists of the brand strategy and the marketing programs. The whole system is supported by a silo-spanning information system that enhances the ability of the organization to share insights and best practices leading to cross-silo synergies and efficiencies.

The objective here is not to create or describe the optimal planning process for all organizations. Rather, the objective is to describe some

FIGURE 4-1

The brand and marketing planning process

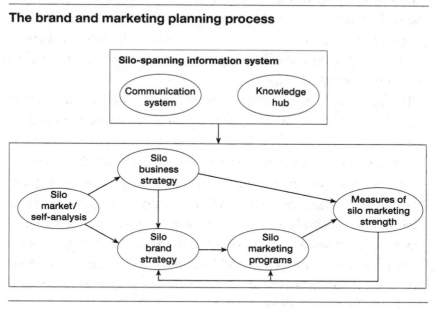

prototype processes and systems that can serve as a model and point of departure for those attempting to develop or refine their own, and to indicate the characteristics of those that have been effective. In that spirit, each of the modules will be described.

Silo Market/Self-Analysis

Input is an analysis of the silo market and the silo organization. The market analysis develops knowledge and insights about the customers, competitors, and market trends. Some questions will be more or less relevant and helpful for a silo business unit. However, having a common starting point and structure will help the silos get on the same page and communicate. The market analysis will feed the articulation of both the business strategy and the brand strategy. The self-analysis proves an objective appraisal of the silo's performance, assets, and competences.

Questions such as the following could structure:

CUSTOMERS

- Who are the largest and most profitable customers? How loyal are they? What are their motivations both functionally and emotionally? What changes in motivations and behavior are being observed? What is the barrier toward making less profitable customers more attractive? Would new products or new positioning help?

- Could the market be segmented around variables such as benefits, usage level, applications, organizational type, customer loyalty, price sensitivity, life stage, lifestyle, purchase drivers, motivations, and so on? How does that segmentation inform the silo brand portfolio strategy?

- What are the motivations, dissatisfactions, and unmet needs of the various segments? Do customers value global reach or local connection? A systems solution or best of breed?

COMPETITORS

- Who are the competitors and potential competitors?

- What are the strength, weakness, and business strategy of the major competitors or groups of competitors? What are the white space opportunities afforded by their weaknesses and strategy?

- What brand equities do they possess? What is their brand portfolio strategy? What are their brand vulnerabilities?

- What trends are they betting on?

MARKET TRENDS

- What are the growth dynamics of the category and subcategories?

- What are the current and emerging cultural, demographic, technology, and economic trends that could affect the business?

- How is the perception of the product categories changing? What are some emerging product categories or subcategories? What is driving that dynamic?

The silo market analysis, if done in depth, will potentially create information overload. It can be both endless and descriptive, with much useful insight. It is important to use transition concepts that allow the most significant and actionable insights to be identified. Concepts such as insights, issues, strategic imperatives, opportunities, threats, strategic trends, category dynamics, strategic options, and so on are candidates. The set to be used should be ones that would best identify the priority insights that have the potential to provide a platform for the development of the business strategy, brand strategy, and marketing programs.

Self-Analysis

Another input to strategy is an objective analysis of the organization. Creating both a revised business strategy going forward and a winning brand strategy needs to be based on the where the silo unit is. Questions to consider:

- What is the current business strategy? What is the value proposition? How is it working? What are the areas that are going well? Disappointing? Why?

- What are the strengths and weaknesses of the organization?

- What are the important strategic initiatives? How are they progressing? Are others needed?

Silo Business Strategy

The business strategy going forward is included because it is often not an exogenous input to the marketing planning process but something that should be articulated or even developed. It is a key input to the brand strategy. Brand strategy, which drives the marketing programs, needs to reflect and support the business strategy. A silo business strategy should include a description of the product-market investment strategy, the customer value propositions, the assets and competences needed, and the functional strategies.[1]

Product-Market Investment Strategy—Where To Compete

A basic strategy decision for each silo is the business scope—what products and services are to be offered to which markets. Within each product market, there need to be investment decisions such as:

- Invest to grow (or enter the product market).

- Invest only to maintain the existing position.

- Milk the business by minimizing investment.

- Recover as many of the assets as possible by liquidating or divesting the business.

The Customer Value Propositions

Ultimately, the offering needs to appeal to new and existing customers. There need to be value propositions that are relevant and meaningful to the customer and are reflected in the positioning of the offering. To support a successful strategy, the value proposition should be sustainable over time and be differentiated from competitors'. It can involve elements such as providing to customers a good value (Wal-Mart), product line breadth (Amazon.com), innovative offerings (3M), a shared passion (Harley-Davidson), or excellence on a functional attribute (Tide).

Assets and Competencies

The strategic competencies or assets that underlie the strategy often provide a sustainable competitive advantage (SCA) because they are not easy to duplicate. A strategic competency is what a silo business unit does exceptionally well, such as a customer relationship program, manufacturing, or promotion. A strategic asset is a resource, such as a brand name, distribution channel, or installed customer base, that is strong relative to that of competitors.

Functional Strategies and Programs

The functional strategies or programs that could drive the business strategy might include a customer relationship program, brand-building strategy, communication strategy, information technology strategy, distribution strategy, quality program, and manufacturing strategy. The business strategy should specify the priorities for functional area strategies to make the business strategy succeed.

Silo Brand Strategy

The brand strategy has two elements. The first is the brand vision: what the brand should stand for going forward. The second is the brand portfolio strategy: a specification of the portfolio brands and their roles going forward.

Brand Vision

The brand vision ultimately drives the marketing program. It should be one of the centerpieces of the planning process. When it clicks, is spot on, everything else that went before will make sense, and ideas for marketing programs will tumble out. The brand vision provides an articulated description of the aspirational image for the brand. One brand vision model, by no means the only one on which to build, is the brand identity model.[2]

The *brand identity model* provides a vehicle to identify and prioritize the brand identity. *Brand identity* is defined as the aspirational associations for the brand, in contrast to the *brand image*, the current brand associations. Some identity associations will involve changing the image or augmenting it. Others will require enhancing or leveraging existing associations. The brand identity will then drive the marketing strategy and communication tactics.

A brand identity for the Haas School of Business at UC Berkeley, shown in figure 4-2, illustrates this model. Three observations should be made about the Haas brand identity. First, the Hass identity has six

FIGURE 4-2

Brand identity for Haas School at Berkeley

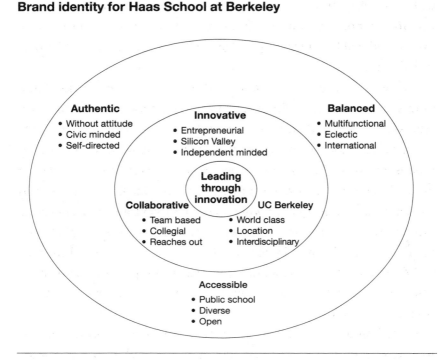

components in addition to the brand essence, shown in the center. Thus, it adapts the view that a brand vision can be and, in fact, should be rich and multidimensional. Most brands have six to twelve dimensions. Second, the model designates three of the six dimensions to be the core identity. These dimensions, usually two to four in number, are the most important and should be the primary drivers of the marketing program. Third, brand essence, "Leading Through Innovation," represents the thrust of the brand identity. The brand essence can contribute understanding, excitement, and even inspiration. However, it is optional—sometimes the core identity provides all the focus and inspiration needed.

To be effective, the brand identity should differentiate from competitors' and resonate with customers and employees. Some identity elements, such as high quality, for example, may be crucial to success but represent points of parity; customers look for acceptable performance on those dimensions. However, the brand identity also needs elements that collectively provide a reason to have a relationship with the brand, perhaps by indicating directly or indirectly functional benefits (innovative), emotional benefits (the prestige of UC Berkeley), or social benefits (collaborative).

An effective brand identity also needs to have substance behind it. It cannot simply be guided by what customers want, but needs to represent what the firm will actually deliver. Toward that end, there needs to be an identification of proof points and strategic imperatives. A *proof point* is an existing program or brand equity element (such as image or loyalty level) that the firm now has. For example, the firm currently may have high perceived quality, which would support a core identity element around high quality. A *strategic imperative* is a program that is essential to make the identity happen. For example, the firm might need an R&D program to generate new products to support a leadership position, or it might need a customer relationship program to create a "friend" position to customers.

In the brand identity model, the brand position is a distinct concept. Its role is to specify the short-term communication objectives to a specified target audience. For the Haas School, the position is around the "Leading Through Innovation" essence and the programs that support it. In general, some components of the brand identity will be aspirational and not ready to be communicated. After programs to deliver on those promises are in place, the position can be altered.

A host of brand frameworks can be used as a basis for planning. Like other elements in the planning process, the brand strategy model should avoid being too simple or too complex. A stripped-down planning system and its output can become shallow and naive. The model should at least have the flexibility to deal with complex contexts. Beware of everything hinging on a magic three-word phrase, or, more generally, forcing a complex brand into a small box. On the other hand, it should not become too complex. It should be understandable. A brand vision model, for example, that has ten overlapping constructs is doomed to generate confusion and frustration. Having said that, the important point is to have a framework that works in the organization. Agonizing over the best one is not usually a good use of resources.

Whatever framework is used in any part of the planning process, it is important that the key concepts be clear and prioritized. Otherwise, they will be used in a superficial or distorted way. Positioning, for example, should be clear. Can it be aspirational? Must it be differentiating? Does there need to be a reason to believe? Is there a format that all should use? Too often people will fill in the blank with some generic generalities that do not really define a strategy and are not actionable. Beware of the positioning statement that is a rambling sentence that says too much.

An alternative brand strategy framework is that used by Unilever. Unilever manages its global brands by what it terms the *brand key*, which describes a brand vision in terms of the benefits it provides, its values and personality, the reasons to believe, its discriminators, and, finally, its brand essence. For each brand, each of these elements is defined and sets a course for the brand and the associated marketing programs.

Another framework, used by a major global firm, has a seven-dimension brand vision template that is a bit different from that of Unilever in that it specifies the scope and segmentation strategy of the brand. It includes the perception of where the brand has permission to compete, core customers (segments, major drivers of preference), value propositions, reason to believe, personality, key point of difference, and brand essence.

GM starts from the premise that a framework such as that of Unilever's brand key suffers from being complex and verbal/left brain oriented. Further, it lacks discipline in that the constructs are often not measured, and the brand aspirations can meander rather aimlessly, becoming a catch-all rather than a clear, focused vision. GM has instead gone to a simple paradigm based on a small set of four to six single-word concepts split between functional descriptors such as safe, economical, smooth performance, and roomy, to emotional and personality descriptors such as spirited, daring, rugged, and contemporary. GM research has shown that customers, employees, and communication partners can discriminate between automobile models, ads, and other marketing programs on the basis of these descriptors. Each word is eventually elaborated using visuals and metaphors so that it has texture and can travel into different cultures. JetBlue Airways uses a similar model where its big five—safety, integrity, caring, passion, and fun—filter all its business decisions.

Brand Portfolio Strategy

Another dimension of brand strategy is brand portfolio strategy, which involves assigning roles to the brands in the silo portfolio. Which are the strategic brands that will support the future business strategies? What brands will provide growth platforms? What brands should have reduced resources committed to them or even be deleted? A process model to address these questions and others will be presented in chapter 6.

In the silo world another perspective is added. Some silo brands, including the corporate brand, may be shared with other silos. For those shared brands, particularly those that have been assigned firmwide strategic brand status, there should be an assessment as to whether the silo brand and marketing programs are enhancing or detracting from the brand equity. Programs that create inconsistencies and potential damage should be identified. They may still be worth pursuing, but the costs to the organization should be visible. Methods to adapt a master brand to the silo context to maintain consistency will be discussed in chapter 5.

Silo Marketing Programs

The brand strategy drives the marketing program, so there is a close link between the two. A silo plan needs to get into the details. How will the brand strategy come to life? What are the major programs that will support and enhance the business strategy?

The marketing program specification should identify themes and centerpiece programs that will span vehicles and lead to integrated communications campaigns. For example, the sponsorship of an auto racing team could be supported by the use of an Internet site to involve the target audience, promotions to leverage and extend the sponsorship impact, and endorsements of racecar drivers connected with the team.

P&G's Pampers has a theme of baby care that drives the Web site that is central to the brand thrust.

Each of the major communication modalities used, such as advertising, sponsorship, viral marketing, Web site strategy, and promotions, should describe the associated marketing program. What is the program? Who is the target? What are the objectives and how will they be evaluated? What is the role of such measures as exposures, customer activities, customer offering experiences, publicity, as well as sale and profits?

The planning process should explicitly call out the opportunities and plans for cross-silo marketing programs. When there is a slot in the plans for such programs, they are much more likely to be considered.

Measuring Silo Market Strength

Measurement drives behavior. Thus, a key lever for a CMO is to get control of the measurement of the performance of the silo units. If the brand strategy is to drive marketing programs, a way to bring that to life in the silo world is to have in place measures of the brand, especially if those measures are tied to performance evaluation as they are in many firms.

There are additional reasons why a measurement system will further the agenda of the CMO. First, it creates the basis for a sound analysis of the strength of the silo business, which becomes an important input to the development of brand strategy. Second, measurement is also integral to effective professional management. A CMO goal should be to improve the consistency of the professionalism of the silo units, and measurement can make a real difference. Finally, there is a need to create effective marketing programs, and a measurement system should also be in place to identify those programs that are getting results and those programs that are not.

Yet many firms lack a measurement system or have a limited one that is used only to track response to advertising. There may be resistance to the cost, or, more likely, there is no consensus brand identity to guide the measures.

The Frito-Lay story is instructive. When Roger Enrico, later CEO of PepsiCo, became head of Pepsi's Frito-Lay unit, he basically spent a year correcting a quality problem throughout the world. He then instituted a "marketplace P&L" that had three components: product equity (blind taste tests), customer equity (measures of distribution), and brand equity (consumer perceptions and attitudes). The goal was to augment financial performance measures that had become excessively influential with what were for him three keys to marketplace success. To gain the acceptance of country managers, the cost was subsidized at the outset. Because of its power to influence programs, the Pepsi CEO decided to make it mandatory across the firm. The marketplace P&L also facilitated communication and empathy among the country managers because they could compare performance measures and discuss the impact of specific programs on these measures.

What to measure? What dimensions? Financial measures of the health of a silo business such as sales, market share, margins, and profit should be in place. The dynamics of such bottom-line measures will be important performance indicators. However, such measures, even if projected, do not always reflect future health. Further, they lack diagnostics that will provide insights directed at improving performance.

Performance measurement thus needs to augment financials with other measures such as perceptions of the silo brands and customer loyalty indicators. Perceptions of the brand are particularly powerful because they tend to have a direct link to the actions of marketing programs and because they can provide a rich picture of the equities of the brands. The practical question arises: what exactly should be measured? Although any set of measures will need to be augmented by silo-specific measures, there are some basic dimensions that should be considered such as:

- *Awareness.* Is the brand well known in the marketplace? What is the unaided awareness among key segments?

- *Reputation.* Is the brand well regarded in the marketplace? Does it have high perceived quality? Is it perceived to be a leader?

- *Differentiation.* Does the brand have a point of differentiation? A personality? Does or could it deliver emotional or self-expressive benefits?

- *Perceived value.* Does the brand strategy deliver better value than competitors'?

- *Energy.* Does the brand have energy? Or is it tired and bland?

- *Personality.* Does the brand have a personality? How should it be described?

- *Relevance.* Is it relevant for today's customers and today's applications? For what product categories or subcategories could the brand lose relevancy?

- *Loyalty.* Are customers loyal to the brand? How large is the loyal group? Who is this group? How do they differ from the general customer base? On what is the loyalty based?

A host of measurement systems can provide different points of departure, such as the systems used by Brand Japan, Y&R, and brand personality scales.

Brand Japan. The project by Nikkei Business Publications (NikkeiBP)—started in 2000 to measure annually the top brands in Japan in both the business-to-consumer (B2C) and the B2B spheres, using about fifteen questions tapping five dimensions—provides another starting point. The dimensions included:

- Loyalty (liked, used, cannot get along without it)

- Quality (reliable, safe, beneficial, relevant)

- Stylish (high status, good looking, unique)

- Warm (familiar, approachable, close)

- Innovative (open up new areas, innovator)

Y&R Brand Asset Valuator. Y&R, which has measured brand equity globally for well over a decade, focuses on four dimensions:

- *Differentiation.* Is the brand different from competitors'?

- *Relevance.* Would this be a brand that you could consider buying?

- *Esteem.* Is the brand held in high regard?

- *Knowledge.* Do you have knowledge about this brand?

Y&R has recently added another variable: energy or energized differentiation, motivated by the observation that most brands are losing esteem, trust, and awareness and the few brands that are creating value—such as Google, Apple, and Nike—are perceived as innovative and dynamic.[3]

Brand Personality Brand personality provides a road to differentiation and a basis for customer relationships. A general personality scale, developed by Stanford researcher Jennifer Aaker, being used by GM and other firms includes fifteen traits organized into five general dimensions—the big five:[4]

- Sincerity (down-to-earth, honest, wholesome and cheerful)

- Excitement (daring, spirited, imaginative, and up-to-date)

- Competence (reliable, intelligent, and successful)

- Sophisticated (Upper-class and charming)

- Ruggedness (outdoorsy and tough)

In Japan and Spain, there is no rugged (Harley-Davidson) dimension, but there is a serenity dimension in Japan and a passion dimension in Spain.[5]

The measurement system should be diagnostic as well as descriptive. Schlumberger, known primarily for its oilfield services, developed a global measurement system that included diagnostics on customer loyalty and specific areas of satisfaction with the company's products, services, and solutions. The system thus produced information that provided tangible short-term benefits for satisfying and retaining specific customer accounts.

A key operational issue is the level of influence that the CMO has over the content and execution of the performance measures. A major objective, from the CMO's view, should be to compare silo performance, which implies that at least some portion of the performance scale should be common. A closely related practical issue is whether the measurement system is part of the local budget or part of the central corporate budget. Controlling the budget usually makes it easier to exert influence, and one problem facing CMOs is that budgets are often constrained.

In small markets there needs to be a cost-benefit analysis to justify the expense of a survey, especially one that covers multiple segments. Dell, for example, was not doing measurement in Japan, because the market could not support it. However, even without a survey, the CMO team can determine the health of the brand, if imprecisely, by qualitative methods—by talking to representative customers and retailers.

Measures of brand strength need to be credible both with top management to gain its support and with the finance team so it does not bypass or undercut the brand team. The key is to link marketing programs to brand strength and financial performance using market data. The best route is usually a program of experimentation or "test and learn" (discussed in chapter 7) whereby a marketing initiative is tried in a portion of the market and its impact is observed. Samsung is one firm that buttressed its top management support for brand-building programs by demonstrating their value in market tests.

The Silo-Spanning Information System

Creating or refining a silo-spanning information system is the most basic and nonthreatening element of the CMO's potential initiatives and potentially one of the most effective change agent vehicles. Market information regarding customer insights, trends, competitor actions, technology developments, and best practices are some of the topics that can be accessed through an information system. Internal information about processes and methods, new products and technologies, best internal practices, and strategies and programs are others. Although conceptually simple, an effective silo-spanning information system can be complex, affected by organizational issues, difficult to manage, and involve difficulties associated with the quality and quantity of participation.

An information system has two distinct components. The first is a communication system, the set of mechanisms that encourage and enable people to communication across silos. The second is a knowledge hub, where knowledge is collected, stored, and accessed by people throughout the organization.

The Communication System

Communication can be fostered across silos in a host of ways. All the strategic linking devices, especially formal networks (described in the last chapter), have a role to play. The following profiles a sample of other approaches. A healthy organization will use them all and will systematically measure the extent to which the system is used and how effectively it is affecting strategy and programs.

Knowledge-Sharing Sessions. Formal and informal meetings that span silos not only result in information exchange but create channels of personal communication that can operate after the meetings. Personal links can result in someone's feeling comfortable to call a colleague and opine that a proposed program is crazy or that a problem should be put on the agenda. Such a conversation can stave off a disaster or encourage an initiative. Most companies have in-person meetings that can vary from once a quarter to once every two years. These are often supplemented with telephone meetings. In fact, all of Dell's global teams (e.g., laptops for business, servers for large businesses, etc.) have a conference call every two weeks. Such meetings are a big part of Honda's communication program.

Training. Many training vehicles are motivated in part to create cross-silo relationships that will foster communication. Frito-Lay sponsors a "market university" about three times a year where thirty-five or so marketing directors or general managers from around the world come to Dallas for a week. The purpose is to involve the silos in the language and models of the central marketing group, to foster information networks, to promote brand concepts, to break down the "I am different" trap, and to plant the seeds of cooperation. During the week, case studies are presented on tests of packaging, advertising, or promotions that were successful in one country or region and then applied successfully in another country. These studies demonstrate that practices can be transferred even in the face of a skeptical local marketing team.

Personal Contact/E-mails. The ultimate information transfer comes from person-to-person contact because attention to nuances, elaboration of ideas, credibility checks, and follow-on back-and-forth discussions are part of the experience. There is really nothing that can replace them. The challenge is to make this transfer happen and to find ways to scale it so that the information spreads among those who could benefit from it. That means that there needs to be a social network, a supporting culture, and motivated participants. All of these come together at Toyota.[6]

One cornerstone of Toyota's success is the open sharing of know-how and expertise via personal communication. There is a curiosity, an eagerness to listen to the ideas of others, whether they be shop-floor workers, dealers in small communities, or coworkers. Few managers reach the senior ranks if they are not good listeners. Further, the interchange is based on a freedom to reject unwise policies from upper management in favor of more defensible options and the openness to hearing bad news or negative feedback up the chain of command. The result is an environment of energetic personal interchange.

Indicators of this culture abound at Toyota. Different functional teams sit together in a large room, which looks uncomfortable but does foster open communication and teamwork. The effort to engage in dialogue with dealers is reflected in five channels used by the Lexus U.S. team. These include fireside chats, where the head of Lexus U.S. and the executive team meet with the top dealers in twelve different locations; and semiannual three-day meetings of the National Dealer Advisory, where the opinions and requests of local dealer associations are recorded.

This type of information flow will benefit from a culture of sharing (versus hoarding) of information. Goldman Sachs, for example, expects that people will pass on insights, experiences, and market knowledge to others who could benefit from it. In fact, an executive who failed to pass on useful information would be chastised. Creating such a culture involves finding visible role models and positioning the need inside a broader information system.

Hands-on Field Visits. Hands-on field visits provide an intimate look at best practices. Honda sends teams to "live with best practices" so that they understand in depth how they work. Other firms send individuals at the CEO level (Henkel and Sony) or the brand staff level (IBM and ExxonMobil) to detect and communicate best practices and to energize the country teams. Seeing best practices firsthand provides a depth of understanding often not achieved by descriptive accounts.

A Planning Staff. P&G uses a worldwide, strategic-planning staff of three to twenty people for each category to encourage and support global strategies. One of the staff's tasks is to tap into local knowledge to learn the consumer and market insights gained from market research and business experience in each country and to disseminate that information globally. Another task is to discover effective country-specific marketing efforts, such as positioning strategies, and to encourage testing elsewhere. Still another is to develop global sourcing strategies. The team also develops policies that dictate which aspects of the brand strategy are the responsibility of global, as opposed to local, management.

The Knowledge Hub

A *knowledge hub*—an organized repository of data, experience, case analyses, and insight—can provide a sustainable asset by putting useful information at people's fingertips. It has the potential to make information handling and exchange productive, easy to use, and efficient. MasterCard, a firm that was early in its appointment of a "knowledge-sharing facilitator" to identify and disseminate best brand practices, credited the program with leveraging the very effective "Priceless" advertising campaign (which describes emotional moments which are priceless—MasterCard is for the rest) across some ninety-six country silos.[7]

Prophet, a brand-based strategy consulting firm mentioned earlier, has a knowledge hub that includes:

- *Case studies*—both internal and external

- *Resources and templates*—research resources, graphics and templates, stock art

- *Learning center*—about Prophet, skills training, brand raps (open forums about a client engagement)

- *Thought leadership*—presentations from Prophet speakers, articles and books by Prophet authors, proprietary studies

- *Industry information*—research and reports, articles and quotes, competitive intelligence

Ernst & Young has developed "The Branding Zone," a global network of information related to marketing strategies, brand positions, visual presentation guidelines, marketing intelligence, and best practices. The goal is to connect globally and instantaneously.[8] The visual guidelines, with templates and an image library, were estimated to save the firm about $7 million to $10 million a year.

Intel has the Brand Builder Intranet site where people can go to understand the management of the Intel brand. In addition to visual presentation guidelines, the site provides guidance for branding innovations—when it should be a branded feature, a subbrand, or a new brand. The site brings the brand to life by describing not only its vision but also its heritage and its relationship to corporate values.

Even with an easy-to-use system, getting participation is always a challenge. Some feel that learning to use even a user-friendly system will take an excessive amount of time and effort and invite frustration. Others feel that the payoff to access the system is simply inadequate to warrant being a participant. Still others who use the system feel buried and confused by too much information. It is helpful to have a person involved, perhaps a knowledge manager, who people can use to get guidance about how to locate information. However, getting usage participation will ultimately rest with the ability of the system to prove its effectiveness.

What can be done to increase usage? To make it more widespread? Some of the things that Prophet has done include:

- *Rewarding those who participate.* Prophet recognizes the most prolific poster and the most popular author each month. There are periodic contests by silo offices as to the posting effort. There is even a pizza lunch "postalooza" contest. Participation for some is tied to the Balanced Scorecard.

- *Capitalizing on newly developed case studies.* When a case study is developed for a client, Prophet makes sure that the resulting report is put into the hub.

- *Reducing information overload.* The firm created a simple path to information, along with an effective search engine. Further, a "best of" section was added to each part of the hub so that people need not slog through all of the content. When all else fails, the knowledge manager is available to help people navigate.

- *Highlighting the new content.* A monthly newsletter summarizes what is new. A "News You Can Use" section highlights a recent practical item. A new-article section describes new articles.

- *Initiating new employees.* When new people join the firm, they are taken on a tour through the Web site, and it is set up as the default home page.

- *Creating liaison roles in each silo.* A liaison is a person in a silo group who can help the silo people access the knowledge hub and who will encourage participation. In another context, the U.S. Army uses analysts who are placed in silo units to find information to support their idea collection system termed CALL (Center for Army Lessons).

- *Including human-interest material.* This information makes the site more interesting (just as the comics make a newspaper more appealing). There are birthday announcements, job changes, and pictures of employees in all sorts of settings, some stimulated by a picture contest.

The Payoff

Recall the discussion at the outset of the chapter. There are two motivations to generate a common planning process and information system—both aimed at making marketing more effective in a silo world. These motivations should be used to evaluate the results.

The first is to enable cross-silo communication by providing common frameworks, vocabulary, measures, and information. The CMO can assess the degree to which such commonalities have been achieved and barriers to communication have been reduced. The assessment can go on to measure communication and see if there are patterns in the nature and quantity of information flow that are occurring.

The second was to upgrade the professionalism of the silo marketing groups. Are they strategic? Can they turn their strategy into tactical programs and implement those programs competently? The presence of a common planning process and information system provide a basis for a dispassionate assessment of the quality of silo marketing management.

For Discussion

1. Evaluate your planning system. Is it common across silos?

2. Evaluate each component. Is it effective, or does it need improvement?

3. Is the communication across silos flowing? What is working and not working?

4. Is the knowledge hub performing? Are there gaps? How is the participation?

Chapter 5

Adapt the Master Brand
to Silo Markets

*Things alter for the worse spontaneously, if
they be not altered for the better designedly.*

—Sir Francis Bacon

*[On how a block of stone could become a lion]
It's easy, I simply get a chisel and chip away
anything that doesn't look like a lion.*

—Pablo Picasso

THE FOLLOWING SCENARIO is all too common. A firm will
have several silo-spanning brands, including a corporate
brand. With no incentives to do otherwise, each silo draws on the
brand's equity to further its own business. Silo executives may not realize that their use of the brand could cause damage by changing its image
or its relationship with the customer. Or they may not care, given the
scorecard. The result is an inconsistent, confused brand. Customers get
conflicting messages and employees and brand partners find it difficult
to build programs and make emotional commitments.

An obvious solution is to have a standardized brand and supporting marketing programs across all silos. When that works, the brand will likely be able to achieve consistency in look, feel, and message. In addition, the chances of creating synergistic marketing programs will be enhanced, and the organization will be more likely to rally around the brand promise. Standardized brands are attractive and a goal or dream for many firms.

However, the same brand everywhere solution can inhibit silos from developing strong brands in their own markets—the ultimate objective. Further, it can be resisted by the silos, creating organization stress. There are situations in which a standardized brand is not optimal or even feasible because it cannot deliver a winning position in a silo market. In that case, there needs to be a process to adapt a master brand so that it has traction in each silo market while still maintaining consistency to its core values.

The chapter begins with a discussion of the power of a standardized brand—the same brand everywhere. Understanding its advantages is important not only because it can be an option but also because it provides a point of departure for approaches to adaptation. The second section explores contexts in which a standardized brand would not be optimal or even make sense. The third introduces five approaches to adapting a master brand to silo contexts. Whether a standardized or adapted master brand is utilized, there needs to be a process to develop the master brand strategy. The final chapter section compares the top-down with a bottom-up process of generating a strategy for a silo-spanning brand.

Standardizing the Master Brand

A master brand that is the same everywhere is an understandable goal. That means the same offering, positioning, advertising, brand-building programs, Web sites, and so on, with only local adaptation to reflect the language, the culture, and the legal settings. For a packaged good, it would mean the same product and packaging. For a service company, it would mean the same customer relationship programs. Brands that have or apparently have achieved the goal are envied—brands such as Heineken, Gillette, Dove, Sony, Vodafone, BP, De Beers, Pampers, and IBM. Having a clear, compelling master brand will generate a consistent message, an internal compass, synergistic programs, and compelling global economies.

Consistent Message. A prime benefit of achieving commonality in a brand across silos is that the brand will be enhanced in each setting rather than becoming confused or, worse, damaged. That is particularly true when there is overlap in the customer base across silos. So if a Toshiba computer customer gets exposed to Toshiba HDTVs or Toshiba Medical Imaging equipment, or if an American Express customer in France gets exposed to an American Express brand-building campaign in the United Kingdom, for example, a consistent message will have an enhanced impact, and an inconsistent message may have a destructive effect.

Internal Compass. The internal brand can be as important as the external brand. If the employees are not on the same page, the brand will find it difficult to achieve its identity. It is hard to live the brand if it is all over the place. If the brand attempts to be premium in one market and value in another, for example, the organization may find it more difficult to deliver behind the promise. With a clear and compelling common brand vision, the organization can more easily manage strategic initiatives, brand extensions, marketing program choices, and on and on. And it is more feasible to manage touch points throughout the silo world so that they are on brand.

Consider the power of the brand vision for the Haas School of Business, put in place in 2005, that was introduced in chapter 4. The brand essence, "Leading Through Innovation," was inspirational, and stimulated and positioned a host of programs throughout the silo units that operate under the Haas umbrella. Haas developed around seven or eight courses under the innovation banner, including one on creativity and innovation in marketing and another on innovation on services. The school-sponsored journal, *CMR*, created a special innovation issue, with fifteen articles written by Haas faculty, and sponsored a one-day symposium on innovation. The entrepreneurship center and curriculum enjoyed a more central role at the school, as did its entrepreneurship forum. The school established the Center for Open Innovation, a research and thought leader force for open innovation; and the Institute for Business Innovation, which will move the innovation curriculum forward. The faculty hiring process was affected. The whole school, including its silo units, became more focused and energized.

Synergistic Programs. Commonality also can create synergy in brand-building programs. Resources used to create winning marketing programs, which could involve customer insights as well as program development, can be shared across silos. Perhaps some localization might be needed, but the bulk of the effort may apply. Further, the implementation of marketing programs is likely to become more efficient as the commonality increases because of scale economies and experience effects.

Compelling Global Economies. The assumption that a standardized brand is good strategy in the global context gained widespread credence because of Ted Levitt's classic 1983 *Harvard Business Review* article titled "The Globalization of Markets."[1] Levitt argued that standardization will be the strategy of successful global firms for three reasons. First, there is a homogeneity of consumer tastes and wants across countries because the forces of communication, transport, and travel are breaking down the insulation of markets. Second, customers will be willing to sacrifice preferences to obtain lower prices that global firms with standardized products and brands could deliver. Third, the economics of simplicity and standardization, especially of products and communication, represent compelling competitive advantages over those that would cling to localized strategies—an argument that applies to cross-product silos as well as country silos. The article provided an academic underpinning to the logical premise that standardization should be the goal of a global business. His article created pressure for firms to maximize sameness everywhere. Many of the same themes appear over twenty years later with Tom Friedman's book *The World Is Flat*. In Friedman's world everyone is connected and collaboration is the norm.[2]

Because of the benefits of standardization, there must be good reason to depart from it. P&G strives to create brands that are virtually identical across country silos, and has probably achieved close to that with maybe a dozen of its eighty-five-plus major brands. Pringles, for example, stands for "fun," a social setting, freshness, less greasiness, resealability, and the whole-chip product everywhere in the world. Further, the Pringles package, symbols, and advertising are virtually the same globally. When such commonality results in strong local offerings and meaningful synergies, there can exist a powerful competitive advantage based on creating a strong market presence, a host of marketing efficiencies, and a more professional and flexible marketing management.

Adapting the Master Brand—Why and When

While standardization will maximize synergy and leverage, it is not always the best or even a feasible route. There is a need to have strong marketing and brand entries in each silo market. In particular, the brand that is driving the purchase and defining the use experience in each product market should be relevant and differentiated as well as visible.

The brand facing customers in a silo market should be relevant to the customers; they should consider it an option when a need arises. If a customer in Germany needs a rental car, they should believe that Hertz is a viable option. They should not exclude it because it is perceived to have the wrong type of cars or to have an aura or personality with which they are uncomfortable. If a high-end customer in Los Angeles is looking for a financial adviser, a bank such as Wells Fargo would not want the customer to believe that it is a consumer bank and thus less relevant for a private bank client. The "one brand for everyone" strategy may sacrifice relevance in some silo markets.

The silo brand also should have some point of differentiation or advantage, some reason to consider and buy. It is not enough to know that the brand represents a large, successful, innovative company such as

Toshiba, GE, or Ford when a specialized product is involved, such as flat screen TV, wind-generated energy, or hybrid cars. The question is not whether the standardized brand will be an adequate choice, but whether it is somehow the best choice. And if there are other options, perhaps smaller firms that have innovated in a product area or a local firm with a heritage in a country, there is no reason to select the big company name.

An established corporate or other master brand may be strong on a lot of dimensions but still not deliver on the relevance and differentiation dimensions, and thus may be relegated to the number-three or -four position in the market. So there is a dilemma of sorts because creating new brands to deliver relevance and differentiation can lead to unbridled brand proliferation, diffusion of marketing effort, and market confusion. One solution is to find ways to adapt the master brand to silo markets.

A misconception that inhibits and distorts the CMO role is that brands and marketing should aim to be the same everywhere or at least involve a very high level of standardization. The entry of a strong CMO is too often thought to be a recipe for mediocrity or even failure in markets in distinctive silo markets.

A move to centralize some aspects of the marketing program does not mean the goal is the standardization of the brand and marketing program. In fact, the level or extent of standardization—the degree to which marketing is the same across silos for brand strategy, positioning, advertising, promotions, channel strategy, packaging, pricing, and so on—is a key variable in centralized marketing management. True, one objective of the CMO is to encourage synergies across silos and leverage good insights and ideas. If successful, that encouragement will result in increased standardization of marketing across silos. However, in many cases, there will also be differences, usually substantial, in marketing across silos even when the CMO has traction and influence.

A CMO position implies that a firm is involved in multiple product markets that could benefit from an overall marketing and branding strategy. It does not or should not imply that the brand and marketing programs everywhere should be identical. The goal should be strong brands and offerings and effective and efficient marketing, not sameness.

In fact, contexts in which a brand is or should be the same everywhere are not common. Even in the Pringles case, the brand is not identical across countries, because some elements, such as flavors, are adapted to local tastes. And Starbucks, a model of standardization, offers beer in some Japanese outlets. Yet, too often, executives, especially those without a marketing background, erroneously assume that a master brand must be a standardized brand. As a result, impatient management often creates by edict the policy that the brand should be the same everywhere, and only "global" brand-building programs are to be used. Although having a standardized master brand may be desirable when potential synergies can be realized, a blind stampede toward that goal can be the wrong course and even result in brand damage in silo contexts plus considerable organizational stress. Silo executives facing what to them are brand decisions that significantly weaken their own brand asset and marketing position can become disillusioned and frustrated. The result can prevent the goals of standardization from being realized.

Consider the following three realities.

First, economies of scale and scope in supporting a standardized brand often may be exaggerated or, in some contexts, may not exist at all. The promise of media spillover is sometimes oversold. There are, in fact, few cross-country media vehicles such as MTV, Eurosport, and the World Cup, and even these have local adaptation. Using a single package design may not result in meaningful added savings. Further, creating localized communication can sometimes be less costly and more effective than adapting "imported" executions. Even an excellent global agency or other communication partner may not be able to execute as well as the local "hot" communication firm.

Second, the brand team may not yet have the organizational capability to be able to find a standardized brand strategy and marketing that will win everywhere, assuming they exist. They might lack the people, the information, the creativity, or the executional skills, and, therefore, end up settling for the mediocre. Finding a superior strategy in one silo context is challenging enough without imposing a constraint that the strategy be used everywhere. Further, even if the optimal "home run" strategy is found, it might not be distinguished from mediocre strategies. Excellence is not always easily recognized.

Third, a standardized marketing and branding strategy simply may not be optimal or feasible when fundamental differences exist across markets. Consider the following instructive contexts where standardization across silos would make little strategic sense.

- *Different market share positions.* Ford's European introduction of a new van, the Galaxy, in the United Kingdom and Germany was affected by its market share position in each country. In the United Kingdom, where Ford was the number-one car brand, the challenge was to expand the market beyond soccer moms to the corporate market. The U.K. Galaxy became the "nonvan," and its roominess was compared to first-class airline travel. In Germany, where Volkswagen was the dominant brand, the Galaxy became the "clever alternative," which positioned it against the VW. HP can make a leadership and innovation claim with more validity in printers where it has a large market share than in other categories where it may be weak or just entering.

- *Different government contexts.* The Galaxy also faced in the United Kingdom (and not in Germany) the fact that because of the tax structure, corporations supplied cars to their employees as a way to provide compensation with less onerous taxes. As a result, a model with the price range of the Galaxy needed to appeal to corporate buyers or not be relevant to a major segment of buyers of vehicles in the Galaxy price range. A soccer moms position would not work, but the "first-class" travel provided a rationale for the inclusion of a van among the acceptable vehicles to buy.

- *Different brand images.* Honda means quality and reliability in the United States, where it has a legacy of achievement in the J.D. Power ratings, but in Japan, Honda is the car-race participant with a youthful, energetic personality. In the U.S. market, leveraging racecar experience would not fit. Heineken is everywhere a social brand representing acceptance among a small group of attractive, upscale people, whereas in its home country, it is a large mainstream brand. Shiseido similarly is upscale everywhere except in Japan, where it is an umbrella to a wider spectrum of products. In fact, in Japan, Shiseido introduced a premium brand because the Shiseido brand did not work at the highest price points. The HP Plus, a global program designed to move HP into the systems solutions space, may not have been optimal for the Japanese market, where, unlike in other markets, HP had under 65 percent awareness and very little printer presence. Strategies reflecting different images make the CMO's job more difficult, but being clear and transparent about the strategy will help.

- *Different customer motivations.* P&G's Olay found that in India people wanted lighter-looking skin rather that younger-looking, as was the case in the United States and Europe. Campbell Soups found little demand for ready-to-eat soups in soup-loving Russia and China but did better when they introduced "starter soups." Citigroup faces very different customer motivations in each of its various product offerings such as retail banking, private banking, investment banking and credit cards. It would be a struggle to have a standardized brand work in all contexts.

- *Different distribution channels.* The distribution channel can affect the offering and the marketing strategy. In China, reaching rural areas can involve many levels of distribution, so that it is hard to control the brand using methods that would work in the United States, where the distribution channel tends to be shorter and clearer. In the United States, ice cream is sold in bulk for people to use at home, but in many countries, it is mainly sold on a stick for snacks.

- *Different stages in customer trends.* A brand may not be at the same stage in all countries even though a common customer trend exists in each. The appreciation of wine exists in China but is embryonic and affects the go-to-market strategy of a company such as the E. & J. Gallo Winery—it does not use its premium offerings in the Chinese market. Trends toward health and healthier eating are farther along in the United States than in many other countries. McDonald's sells both gourmet coffee and hamburgers, both at very different points on the maturity scale and needs to adopt the McDonald's brand to target audiences.

- *Different social economic stage.* For some markets, such as in rural India, most products and brands sold in the West are simply irrelevant. When an area lacks electricity or when it is unreliable, the product profile and attribute preferences change dramatically. Or when the household budget is a small fraction of that in developed countries, constraints dictate buying habits.

- *Strong local heritage.* Nestlé and Unilever often retain an acquired local brand simply because there is significant customer loyalty based on the brand's heritage and connection to the local community that could not be transferred to a global brand. Relationships with local brands can be powerful especially in contexts in which the incidence of advertising is low and the historical relationships therefore take on more weight.[3]

- *Different cultures and work practices.* Wal-Mart's surprising failure in Germany was in part due to the company's inability to adjust to a very different culture and work environment.[4] The short shopping hours in Germany and the fact that Germans did not want assistance in the store were just a few of the conditions to which Wal-Mart had trouble adjusting. Wal-Mart's failure in Germany and the fact that it is weak elsewhere in the world makes visible the difficulty of exporting even successful business models, especially one based on scale. Landor and other design firms struggle to have the same umbrella brand that provides credibility for their creative, artistic offerings and also with analytic, strategic consulting.

- *Preempted positions.* A superior position for a chocolate bar is to own the associations with milk and the image of a glass of milk being poured into a bar. The problem is that different brands have preempted this position in different markets—for example, Cadbury in the United Kingdom and Milka in Germany. So in those countries, this position would not be an option for Nestlé.

- *Different customer responses to executions and symbols.* There are tactical concerns as well. A Johnnie Walker ad in which the hero attends the running of the bulls in Pamplona was effective in some markets, including Spain, but seemed reckless in Germany and too Spanish in other countries. The attitude toward diet drinks and food outside the United States is very different and is one reason that *light* instead of *diet* is seen on food products. The business community has a different way of appraising small copiers than do people considering a product for their home. The Wells Fargo stagecoach plays differently with a retail banking customer than an investment bank client.

The pendulum now is swinging toward making sure that the firm understands and is effective in local markets. Sir Martin Sorrell, the CEO of WPP, the holding company for dozens of leading communications firms and one of the leading proponents of standardization during the past two decades, has argued that pressure for commonality went too far.[5] His office is shifting its attitude and worrying about such issues as how to approach Muslim consumers (over 25 percent of the world's population) and what the driving trends in Asian markets are. Sir Martin notes that a decision by a global firm to kill a country brand that was generating 30 percent of the profits within that country was not necessarily the way to build a viable country business. He suggests that the shift of power to central managers should be reversed.

Brand standardization across silos is a worthwhile goal and should not be resisted because of assumptions of barriers that are illusionary or that could be overcome. When superior brand strategies and tactics work across silos, they should be employed. However, standardization should occur only when it makes sense in that it furthers the goal of having strong brands and marketing programs in all markets. The goal of global brand management is to have strong rather than the same brands and marketing programs.

Adapting the Master Brand—How

A strong corporate brand, such as Disney or Sony, or a strong master brand, such as Disney's ESPN or Sony's VAIO, is often asked to play across a lot of silo markets. Toshiba, for example, is used across well over one hundred product silos and over one hundred countries as well. The challenge is to make that master brand relevant, differentiated, and energized in the silo markets. There are five ways to adapt the master brand, as shown in figure 5-1.

Create Relevant Silo-Spanning Associations

One advantage of a master brand is that it has the resources to create visibility and strong associations. With resources, a master brand can generate major sponsorships and hot-button Internet programs that can

FIGURE 5-1

Adapting the master brand to a silo market

be leveraged over all the silos it touches. The problem is to find associations that work across silos, that generate relevance, differentiation, and/or energy in the silo markets. Some associations that fit those criteria are organizational associations that are well suited for master brands and, in fact, ill suited for most "local" brands, such as being innovative, prioritizing quality, being visibly concerned for customers, acting socially responsible, being global, and being connected to the heritage of a country.

Innovation. Virtually all organizations strive to be perceived as innovative in order to generate both brand energy and credibility for new products. However, achieving an innovative reputation is not easy; in fact, few firms break out of the clutter on this dimension. R&D spending, a host of patents, and even a stream of new products will not necessarily enhance the brand. There are some guidelines. First, innovation should be credible, relevant, and visible. The firms that have pulled it off, such as Sony, Apple, and Nintendo, usually have highly visible branded new offerings that capture the imagination of the public. Second, there is a lot of inertia in the perceptual marketplace. Sony is still considered highly innovative despite the fact that its innovation record in the last fifteen years or so has not been exemplary. So an innovation reputation will endure and thus be all the more worthwhile. Third, it is easier to be innovative with many product silos as long as that innovation is captured by a brand, simply because there is more product energy than in one silo.

Perceived Quality. Perceived quality is important in all settings. If it is high, the brand is likely to be highly rated on other attributes. Perceived quality is one of the few brand attributes that has been shown to influence ROI and stock return.[6] However, perceived quality is even more difficult to achieve than perceived innovation, as illustrated in the experience of Cadillac and Buick, which failed to get credit for exceeding the quality levels of Mercedes. Delivering actual quality is not enough; perceptions should be managed as well, which means that quality cues such as the thickness of the ketchup, the dress of the airline cabin attendants, or the appearance of a bank statement should be understood and actively managed. Still, it can take years for improvements in actual quality to be reflected in perceptions.

Concern for Customers. The relationship between a brand and its customers spans silos and is a key determinant of loyalty and thus long-term profitability. A brand that exudes a concern for customers and delivers on that dimension has the basis for a strong customer relationship. Firms such as Nordstrom and Singapore Airlines have created significant loyalty based on a visible, enthusiastic effort to please customers. Customer concern is another value that nearly all firms aspire to have. They all talk the good talk. To gain the desired reputation, firms often need some visible, over-the-top programs, preferably branded programs. Some legendary stories can also help—such as how Nordstrom once took back a defective tire even though it never sold tires, or how a FedEx employee once hired a helicopter to maintain service quality.

Citizenship—Good Company Vibes. What kind of people and values are behind this corporate brand? People and organizations prefer to do business with those they respect and admire. Is the organization "good people" with a perspective beyond a preoccupation of enhancing shareholder value at all costs? Is the company concerned about the employees, the community, education, participating with fighting and coping with disease, the larger society problems, and the environment? Companies such as HP and Johnson & Johnson have engendered respect for their values that has resulted in positive attitudes and loyalty even during times in which their products were challenged.

A visible dimension of citizenship through being environmentally sensitive and responsive is important to a growing influential segment, especially in Europe. Evidence from a U.K. study supports this conjecture, at least when the industry is visible and the corporate brands are differentiated.[7] Both Shell and BP developed an environmental friendly brand in part because of their visible investment in renewable energy sources. Esso, in contrast, took the principled position that renewable energy was not a viable solution and, further, that the Kyoto accords on the environment were flawed and should be opposed. As a result, a high-profile Stop Esso campaign coordinated by Greenpeace attacked Esso. A subsequent poll done by Greenpeace found that the proportion of British gasoline buyers who say they regularly use Esso stations dropped by 7 percent during the year of the campaign.

Being Global. Being global generally implies that the firm behind the brand is both successful and a leader, which in turn implies that it will be innovative and create quality products. A global brand can also deliver self-expressive benefits, especially in categories such as fashion clothing and high-end autos,

The power of global associations was demonstrated by a study that involved qualitative interviews with 1,500 consumers in over forty-one countries, followed by a quantitative survey that included a preference scale of three leading brands in six product categories.[8] The result showed that associations with being global influenced preference, and suggested why. The fact that consumers believe that global brands have higher quality in part because they tend to have the latest innovations accounted for 44 percent of the variance in preference. Two other associations connected with "global"—the prestige of being global and having social responsibility—also influenced preference but much less so (12 percent and 8 percent, respectively) than the quality dimensions.

A Country Association. When the CMO is creating a global brand strategy, a key decision is whether to emphasize the country association. A country association is usually a potential source of differentiation because most competitors will be from other countries—the Japanese option or the German option can be unique. It can also be a source of credibility if the country is perceived to have skills in the product class. Thus German cars, Swiss watches, Italian pasta, or English sweaters all start with some perceived quality. A country association can also add prestige. Western brands such as Mercedes, Louis Vuitton, Burberry, Nike, Levi's, Starbucks, McDonald's, British Airways, and many others are perceived outside the United States or Europe as being prestigious largely because of their country of origin. Of course, being associated with a country can be a negative if that country is perceived as making inferior goods or if it becomes controversial because of a foreign policy over which the brand has no control. A Chinese manufacturer may well feel that the country of origin is a net negative.

It is necessary to focus on a few dimensions of a brand. Attempting to have too many associations can lead to confusion and disinterest. However, it may be possible to stand for both a country and being global when the country link suggests a functional or an emotional benefit and the global association simply adds credibility. In fact, Sony explicitly attempts to make its brand global, Japanese, and, in addition, local. Sony actively works to link to the local country through local events and simply thinking like the locals.

Spin the Brand Story for the Silo Market

Another approach is to have the same brand identity across silos, but to interpret elements of it differently in different countries. So a systems solution might have a different take in a country with a customer maturity different from another's. Or social responsibility could take an educational focus in one country and support the arts in another. Or the innovation story could take one form for the home computer market and another for the television market.

ChevronTexaco has a core brand identity that consists of four values: clean, safe, reliable, quality. The silo markets hold workshops to adapt that brand identity to their context. One mechanism is to interpret the core elements in their marketplace. So what does quality mean in the context of a convenience store? Or in a lube business? As a result, the silo units do get a degree of flexibility to adapt the brand but within the confines of the overall brand strategy.

Augment with Additional Associations

Still another adaptation strategy is to add associations to the master brand in the silo context. The idea is to add associations to the brand promise for the silo market that will be relevant and even compelling but will not be inconsistent with the global brand.

ChevronTexaco, in addition to allowing the silos to interpret the brand identity elements, allows the silos to add one additional element to the four-element core identity. So the lube business could add performance, and the Asian group could add respectfully helpful. The result is more ability to link with the silo customer. In part because the addition is made in the context of the brand strategy workshop, there is little chance that any added element would be inconsistent with the brand.

One possibility is to add an attribute or benefit that is valued by the silo organization but not by the "rest of the world." One energy company had a well-defined brand that worked throughout the world. However, in a South American country, customers were used to being cheated at the pump and getting less than they paid for. An honest pump was a believable and relevant point of differentiation. What the company added to the brand promise in that country was in no way inconsistent with the global brand promise but, rather, reinforced aspects of it, such as trust.

Another possibility is to add an organizational or personality association that bonds with the silo marketplace. A brand-spanning product silo, for example, could portray an image of being expert and involved in one or more of the silo products. Thus, Nike golf balls might come from an organization that has all the attributes of the Nike organization but also is into golf and passionate about creating good golf balls. The Nike brand may have a weak connection to golf, but the Nike organization in the golf context will have some programs that express the Nike commitment to the sport.

With a country-spanning silo, the brand could add a local or country flavor by adding associations to enable it to connect with the culture and heritage of the country. A brand in the French market, for example, could use a local sponsorship of an arts program or a package modification to link to the French culture. There can be tension between being local and global. However, it is very doable. Sony, in fact, as already noted, has long had the objective of being three things in each market—global, Japanese, and local—the best of all worlds.

Emphasize Different Elements of the Brand Identity

A brand that has a core identity of four or five items can selectively draw from this list to maximize its impact on the silo market. A major financial services company was developing a loan program eventually to be used in many of the countries in which it operated. The brand concepts included in its brand identity were "easy to work with," "bias to yes," "flexibility," and "speed." Qualitative research followed up with a quantitative concept test on three representative countries that showed that the markets reacted very differently. In the United States, "easy to work with" and "bias to yes" were the most effective appeals. However, in an eastern European country, "easy to work with" and "speed" had the most impact, while in an Asian developed country, "flexibility," "easy to work with," and "speed" were the winners. So countries could emphasize different aspects of the identity even though the identity was the same.

Use a Branded Differentiator

The basic challenge is to create credibility and differentiation in the silo market so the brand is considered and eventually preferred. A corporate brand may have a ton of trust and prestige in general, but it still must meet the challenge in a specific product class where competitors are likely to be established. So Chrysler might be highly respected as a brand and as a maker of minivans, but if the customer now wants a hybrid, Chrysler must find a way to be relevant. Toshiba is a great brand, but that does not mean that it will have credibility in a certain product class. The competition may have established a position within a product class that provides a reason for customers to buy and that creates a relevance challenge for others.

A branded differentiator can help. A branded differentiator is an actively managed branded feature, ingredient, technology, service, or program that creates a meaningful, influential point of differentiation for a branded offering over an extended time. So a branded differentiator is more than slapping a brand name on a feature. It should be meaningful, not a trivial difference, and should be actively managed over an extended time with a budget behind it. Target has become credible with over a dozen designer products, such as the Mossimo (Mossimo Giannulli)-designed line of clothing and shoes. The Geek Squad, a branded team of computer installation and service people, provide credibility for Best Buy in the computer service business. Toshiba used its Encompass branded analytical program to gain a position in the document solutions space. Sharp branded its television technology as AQUOS, perhaps attempting to duplicate the decades-long impact that Trinitron tubes had on the Sony television business. In all these cases, the branded differentiation has provided credibility and differentiation in a part of the market where the master brand (Target, Best Buy, Toshiba, or Sharp) may otherwise not be considered.

Top-Down Versus Bottom-Up Processes

When the brand and marketing strategy from the various silos overlap, they need to be reconciled to avoid confusion and inefficiency. In particular, the common aspects of the brand vision should be recognized so that there will be a common base to build the brand. Further, any elements that are unique to one or more silos should not be inconsistent because of the resulting effect on customer perceptions and, perhaps as important, the effect on the task of getting people who are driving the brand and the marketing programs to be consistent. The process question remains—how to do it?

The mechanism to relate master brand strategies to silo brand strategies (the master brand adapted to the silo context) can be either *top-down*, where the master brand strategy is the driver and the silo strategy adapts, or *bottom-up*, where the silo brand strategy evolves into a master brand strategy.

The top-down approach involves developing a master brand strategy that specifies the brand identity, position, and brand-building programs that the organization will employ across silos. The silo managers then take this strategy and adapt it to their contexts, using one of the adaptation approaches.

The top-down approach has advantages. It gets a master brand strategy in place in a timely manner. Because it has the benefit of a broad perspective and vision, it can support the master brand strategy going forward.

A bottom-up approach may never have the perspective needed to chart the optimal master brand course. Sometimes the top-down approach is the only way to achieve a master brand strategy with powerful silo managers who resist any effort to join a coordinated effort. It can be a significant change mechanism, and that may be what is needed. Further, with dozens, if not hundreds, of business units, it may simply be the only practical approach.

A top-down process can be inclusive and involving; it does not have to be developed by the top managers in an isolated tower. One firm developing a top-down strategy involved some twenty people on a team that represented both regions and businesses. As they created drafts of master brand strategies, they went to the worldwide offices and had vigorous discussions. As a result, the regions had real input into the final result, and buy-in was more possible. When Nissan started a similar process, it brought an international team into Tokyo many times over a four-month period to participate in discussions not only on creating the brand strategy but also on analyzing the relevant market trends and forces. The whole firm felt that it had contributed.

The top-down approach can be efficient and achieve a faster final result than the bottom-up route. However, the task is nontrivial and can take time. One reference point is the experience of Fujitsu, which formed a corporate brand office in 2000 after spending two years working on brand management issues. The initial charge was to manage the global guidelines for the use of the name and logo, manage a global brand study, manage the corporate Web sites and approve subsites, authorize (but not implement) global brand-building campaigns, and plan and execute corporate brand strategy globally. The company judged that it took three years to get its corporate brand in place, and still much of the work to coordinate the brand over some five hundred subsidiaries was left to be done.

The bottom-up approach allows the silo managers to create silo brand strategies with few constraints. They create a strategy that gives them the best chance to succeed. The master brand strategy is then built from the silo brand strategies. The silo managers come together and look for commonalities among their silo brand strategies. The common elements become the master brand strategy. Over time, the number of distinct strategies (with variants) usually falls as the silo managers share and adopt experiences and best practices and the master brand strategy becomes more disseminated and successful.

A variant of the bottom-up strategy is to aggregate silos into regions or product categories. The aggregation might, for example, be on the basis of the similarity of the product or market in geographic proximity, customers, product technology, or stage in the product life cycle. Moving from many brand contexts to a limited number can result in a more manageable process and in capturing a substantial portion of potential synergy.

The bottom-up strategy provides the least stress on the organization because the silos are free to create the very best strategy for them. What frequently happens is that they are surprised about the degree of commonality across silos that is created. Because the brand has the same heritage and the offering is similar or identical, that there is much in common should be expected. Nevertheless, most are surprised.

A division of a major firm consisted of four groups, each marketing high-end computers and software. The products of each group were distinctive and were targeted to different market segments. Each group created its own brand identity, believing that its context was unique in significant ways. However, when the groups came together, they were amazed to find how similar their brand identities were. In fact, with some wordsmithery, three of the groups ended up with the same identity, and the fourth only needed to augment the extended identity with one item. This illustrates how the bottom-up approach can drive the organization toward a common identity.

The selection of the best approach for the organization must address a realistic appraisal of the existing planning process, culture, and values. If decentralization is truly a key value and heritage, and the CMO is not playing the role of strategic partner or strategic captain, a top-down approach may not be optimal or even feasible. It also may not be feasible in a merger or acquisition situation where two organizations protect their historical brand heritage but must unify around the ongoing brand. If, however, a committed CEO and a strong CMO team generate urgency about building a master brand strategy, the top-down approach is likely to be best.

For Discussion

1. What brands pursue a standardized strategy? What exceptions in their strategy are likely?

2. Pick a brand such as IBM or Starbucks. Does that brand pursue a standardization strategy? If not, why not?

3. Pick a master brand from your portfolio. Which, of any, of the five adaptation approaches discussed is it using?

4. What are the advantages of the top-down process? Does your firm use top-down or bottom-up? Is that the right approach?

Chapter 6

Prioritize Brands in the Portfolio

*If you find yourself in a hole, the first
thing to do is stop digging.*

—Will Rogers

*Nobody has ever bet enough on a
winning horse.*

—Richard Sasuly, author

MOST CMOS LOOKING AT their organization see too many brands with too few priorities and too little leverage—a context that makes it difficult to create strong brands and effective marketing. It is not uncommon to see hundreds, sometimes many hundreds, of brands fighting for resources and the minds of customers. Adobe, for example, has 90 brands, and Unilever at one point had 1,600 brands covering 100 countries. This overbranding can lead to confusion and diffusion of resources and even to paralysis in branding new offerings.

An overbranded portfolio can result in debilitating confusion. Rather than clarity, there may be brands with complex branding structures that lack logic and consistency. Some brands may reflect product types, and others price-value, and still others customer types or applications. The branded offerings may even overlap. The portfolios can differ over countries. The totality simply reflects a mess. Customers have a hard time understanding what is being offered and what to purchase. Even employees may be confused. Sometimes the confusion is so extensive that the organization is paralyzed—it cannot bring an innovation to market, because it is not clear how to brand it.

Having too many brands also means that there are never enough resources to support the brands. Many, if not all, of the brands get starved as the resources are spread too thin. Worst of all, the strategic brands that represent the future get underfunded and fail to create the equity to support the business going forward.

Two additional challenges facing marketing organizations are closely related to overbranding. One is to identify the priority strategic brands—those that will support the business strategy going forward—and to make sure that all the portfolio brands have well-defined roles. Another is to leverage the strategic brands by taking them into new products and new countries. All three of these challenges are caused in part by an ad hoc brand strategy guided by a silo-based or nonexistence process (see figure 6-1) and addressing them needs to be high on the CMO's agenda.

The silos, particularly product silos, can significantly contribute to the brand proliferation and absence of an effective portfolio strategy. With their heritage of autonomy and entrepreneurship and their narrow silo perspective, they empower those who want to brand the newest offering brought to market. Further, they lack the discipline, expertise, and motivation to develop procedures that would make the case for adding brands more demanding and allow decisions to be made to prioritize and eliminate brands. They simply have other things on their

FIGURE 6-1

Challenges created by silo-based strategies

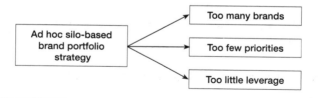

mind. And the lack of prioritized brands inhibits the ability to leverage big brands by expanding their product or country scope. The CMO is eminently well suited to provide the needed processes, discipline, and organization-wide perspective.

These three challenges—too many brands, too few priorities, and too little leverage—are difficult to address because of four factors. First, brand strategy can be ad hoc and silo based. The result is a lack of organization-wide perspective and, ultimately, a parochial and suboptimal strategy. Second, managers tend to have an emotional attachment to their brands and new offerings—which often represent in a very personal way a person's career—that inhibits tough decisions. Third, the decision process involving adding or retaining brands, prioritizing brands, and leveraging strategic brands can be inadequate or nonexistent. Judgments are not stress-tested, and there is too little concern for the total brand portfolio strategy going forward. Fourth, silos can be insular, so that information needed to leverage strategic brands into new products and countries may be lacking.

The good news is that overbranding and the absence of a coherent brand strategy are an obvious problem, if not a crisis. Anyone can count brands, divide that number by the marketing budget, and conclude that the budget will not support that number of brands. In addition, the confusion and lack of priorities are often visible. The bad news is that branding is a very emotional topic for people and groups because brands symbolize power and worth. It therefore becomes important to develop processes and frameworks that encourage objectivity and rigorous analysis.

Developing a brand portfolio strategy in a silo environment involves making the decision to add or eliminate brands, assign roles and establish priorities, and how to leverage the strategic brands. The CMO team should either facilitate or control three frameworks that can help.

- The brand addition framework is a structured process to approve the addition of a brand to the portfolio so that new brands are added only if justified.

- The brand prioritization framework involves an objective, systematic review of the brand portfolio to identify the strategic brands, assign roles to others, and identify those brands that should be deleted or relegated to descriptor status.

- A brand extension framework helps select products and countries into which the strategic brands should be extended.

Too Many Brands—The Brand Addition Framework

Overbranding emerges because there are few restrictions on the introduction of new brands. The way to control brand proliferation is to make the owners objectively justify each new brand. They should demonstrate why an existing brand, which will bring with it significant brand equity, should not be used. An existing brand provides recognition, familiarity, and visibility plus associations on which to build, such as perceptions of quality, brand personality, and functional benefits. Further, putting an established brand on a successful new product will potentially enhance the brand further.

Creating a new brand instead of leveraging existing brands has its place but organizations should do so only after making a disciplined analysis. The analysis should consider four questions that form the brand addition framework:

- Is the business associated with the new brand or subbrand substantial enough, and will it have a long enough life to justify creating or maintaining a brand?

- Would the use of any existing brand inhibit or even detract from the brand promise of the new offering?

- Would the new offering detract from or confuse the message of a candidate brand for the offering?

- Is there a compelling reason to introduce a new brand?

Will the Business Support a New Brand Name?

The potential business should justify the commitment that a new brand represents, particularly if the new brand will not represent a new growth platform to support future offerings. If the business is ultimately too small or short lived to support necessary brand building, a new brand name will simply not be feasible whatever the other arguments are. Estimates of a business's potential and the cost of establishing a new brand tend to be optimistic, driven by the excitement of the business champions. Further, the necessity of maintaining a brand after the introduction phase has long passed is particularly subject to faulty assumptions. There must be not only the means but the will. Many organizations have deep pockets but short arms.

Would an Existing Brand Inhibit or Even Detract from the Promise?

The existing brand can bring a host of assets to the table, as already noted. However, if there is a fit problem, an existing brand can adversely affect the credibility and associations in the new space. Clorox is associated with household cleaning products and bleach, and it could never be used on food products, so brands like Hidden Valley dressings and KC Masterpiece barbecue sauce lead those product silos. Sony and Apple have struggled to extend into the business market, and IBM and HP have similarly struggled to move into the home market, in part because of the brand personality each has fostered. An upmarket offering may be handicapped by a brand that is not suited to deliver self-expressive benefits. Volkswagen, with a heritage of making economical cars, was undoubtedly a handicap in the market performance of the very upscale Phaeton.

Would the New Offering Detract from or Confuse the Message of the Existing Brand?

Will the use of an existing brand on a new offering damage the brand by affecting its perceived quality, product class associations, attribute associations, and so on? Moving a brand into a value segment, for example, can put at risk not only a brand's perceived quality but also its ability to deliver self-expressive benefits. If Tiffany allowed department stores to use the blue box, it would tarnish the symbol of a Tiffany gift. Fuzzing up a product class association can affect a brand's credibility and relevance. Cadbury's association with fine chocolates may have been weakened when it got into other candy products. And a new offering can create inconsistent associations. The Nestlé company, known for its chocolate and as a maker of fine goods such as Nescafé and Nestlé's Carnation products, could never be associated with its pet food line, which is marketed under the Purina umbrella.

Even if a brand is not damaged, the absence of a positive impact of a brand should be a warning sign. Ideally, firms should extend a brand into areas that will give it energy and make it more upscale, more global, more advanced, more reliable, and on and on.

Is There a Compelling Reason for a New Brand?

There should be a compelling reason why firms need a new brand (or subbrand or endorsed brand) to tell its own story, and silo businesses, whether they be those around a high-tech innovation or country silos, tend to have a low bar with respect to "compelling." Being close to the business and emotionally involved, product-driven silo business managers often think that their new offerings are so unique and pathbreaking that they need a new brand. A country manager can overemphasize the attachments to and power of a local brand. Further, the silos too often can look at the existing scope of their business and fail to take a strategic long-term view of the master brand platforms needed to support the future business scope.

Some examples of potentially compelling rationales for separate silo business brands can help illustrate the compelling concept and provide a structure to evaluate proposals or options. However, recognize the biases involved. Because a context fits one of these rationales does not mean that the case is made.

- *Owning benefit or attributes.* A brand may be needed to focus and potentially own a functional benefit. Head and Shoulders dominates the dandruff control shampoo category, while Pantene, "for hair so healthy it shines," a brand with a technological heritage, focuses on the segment concerned with enhancing hair vitality. The total impact of these brands would be lessened if—instead of being distinct brands—they were restricted to the brand "P&G

shampoo" or even were branded as P&G Dandruff Control or P&G Healthy Hair. P&G detergents are similarly well positioned to serve niche markets: Tide (tough cleaning jobs), Gain (with fabric softener), Downy (providing a soft feel and fresh smell), Cheer (all-temperature), and five other brands provide sets of focused value propositions that would be difficult to achieve with a single P&G detergent brand. Although Tide, with a host of extensions (such as Tide Coldwater, Tide with Bleach, Tide to Go), is the largest brand, Gain and Downy have also broken the billion-dollar barrier.

- *Capturing a different personality.* Lettuce Entertain You Enterprises, a Chicago-based restaurant group, has rolled out thirty-nine restaurant concepts since its first restaurant, R. J. Grunts, appeared in 1971. Each restaurant has its own image, personality, style, and brand name. From Shaw's Crab House to Tucci Benucch to Brasserie Jo to the Mity Nice Grill, each is unique and successful. Many are trendy, the ultimate restaurant accolade. Joie de Vivre Hospitality has a group of hotels, each with a different brand and distinct personality, from stuffy European Savoy to rock-fan friendly Phoenix to old San Francisco Rex.

- *Representing an offering that creates a new subcategory.* After we cut through the hype, some new offerings are so innovative that they change the game. If these are not branded, their ability to create advantage may be short lived. And some can even change what people buy by creating a new category or subcategory, such as Asahi Super Dry beer, the Apple iPod, or Toyota's Prius. In that case, a brand may be an indispensable way to own the new space.

- *Resolving a channel conflict.* Channel conflict can force new brands. Fragrance and clothing brands, for example, need different brands to access the upscale retailers, the department stores, and the drug or discount stores. Thus, L'Oréal has Lancôme, L'Oréal, and Maybelline New York cosmetics brands for different channels. The

VF Corporation supports four distinct brands—Lee, Wrangler, Maverick, and Old Axe—in part to deal with channel conflict.

Other Considerations

Here are three additional observations. First, subbrands and endorsed brands provide less independence for the silo business than a new brand, but also less investment—the new subbrand or endorsed brand will be supported by a current master brand. The endorsed brand Miracle fragrance from Lancôme is a brand endorsed by the master brand Lancôme. The role of the endorser brand is to represent an organization providing assurance that the endorsed brand will live up to its claims. Subbrands are brands that augment or modify the associations of a master or parent brand. The subbrands can add associations (Sony Walkman), a brand personality (Callaway Big Bertha), a product category (Ocean Spray Craisins), and even energy (Nike Force). In doing so, they stretch the master brand.

Second, the decision of whether to introduce a new silo brand or subbrand will depend in part on how much customer overlap there is between the core market and the new context, new product line, or new country. If the overlap is low, then the equity of the master brand and the costs and risks of using a new brand (or subbrand or endorsed brand) will tend to be low. In that case, there need not be such a bias toward an existing master brand unless, with a longer time perspective, the overlap might be expected to increase.

Sometimes, however, the customer overlap is hidden or not obvious. For example, when Russia opened up its market, the leading brands turned out to be Western brands that theoretically had no exposure to the Russian people. The appeal and ability of a global brand to penetrate across countries can be surprising. Further, seemingly isolated business units, such as BP's oil drilling business and its retail gasoline, may affect each other. The fact is that B2B buyers are also consumers. Those that make decisions about oil drilling rights also buy gasoline, and it can be helpful if a decision maker is also a satisfied patron of a retail outlet.

Third, a distinction should also be made between different brands and the same brand with different names—P&G's Tide is Ariel in Europe, and they are virtually the same on all dimensions. When the brand is essentially the same in two countries but for linguistic or legal reasons requires a different name, the use of a different name may be of limited importance.

Too Few Priorities—The Brand Prioritization Framework

If the flow of new brands is under control, there still remains the challenge of managing the existing brand portfolio. What can the CMO do if there are too many brands to support and little clarity about brand roles and priorities? It may be clear that pruning would be healthy and setting priorities that span silos is strategically necessary. However, there is a lot of emotion around brands. All brands develop patrons, and it is unusual for anyone in the organization to suggest dumping or even withdrawing support from a brand. And silo organizations are not well equipped with the expertise or political will to make the hard analysis and decisions regarding existing brands. Nor do they have the organization-wide perspective. What may appear to be a priority brand in a silo may not be one from an organizational view that sees more attractive options.

The CMO can thus make the case for a periodic review and pruning of the brand portfolio supported by an objective in-depth analysis that can support tough decisions. A brand portfolio review supported by the Brand Priority Framework or something comparable, can precipitate decisions that are too easily put off. And it can deal with political costs of making tough decisions, often with turf issues. Closing a defense base is virtually impossible because of powerful local politicians unless a neutral, bipartisan national committee with no local ties provides an analysis and recommendations. Similarly, a dispassionate review of the brand portfolio by brand specialists can provide the same decision structure and organizational cover when it is needed.

The first step in the brand priority framework, as shown in figure 6-2 or something comparable, is to determine the relevant brand set to appraise. The second, developing assessment criteria, is followed by brand evaluation, identifying the strategic status of each brand, creating a revised brand portfolio strategy, and, finally, designing a transition strategy.

FIGURE 6-2

Brand priority framework

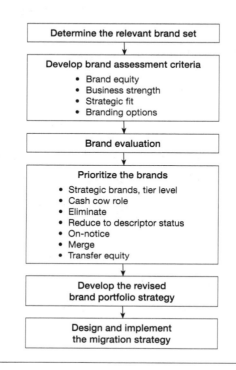

Determine the relevant brand set

Develop brand assessment criteria
- Brand equity
- Business strength
- Strategic fit
- Branding options

Brand evaluation

Prioritize the brands
- Strategic brands, tier level
- Cash cow role
- Eliminate
- Reduce to descriptor status
- On-notice
- Merge
- Transfer equity

Develop the revised
brand portfolio strategy

Design and implement
the migration strategy

Identify the Relevant Brand Set

The brand set will depend on the problem context. It can include all brands and subbrands, of course. However, often the focus will be on a subset: brand groupings of comparable brands. For example, an analysis for GM could include its major nameplates: Chevrolet, Pontiac, Buick, Cadillac, Saab, Saturn, and GMC. Another analysis stage could then be subbrands attached to a master brand. Thus, for Chevrolet, its subbrands in the SUV and van arena would be Uplander, Express, HHR, Tahoe, Trailblazer, Suburban, and Equinox. When brands that share similar roles are involved, it becomes easier to evaluate the relative strength.

Develop Brand Assessment Criteria

If organizations are to establish brand priorities, they need evaluation criteria. These criteria must have metrics so that brands can be scaled.

The point of making the process highly structured and quantified is to provide stimulation and guidance to the discussion and the decision. There should be no illusion that the decision will default to picking the higher number. The criteria will depend on the context, but in general there are four areas or dimensions of evaluation:

BRAND EQUITY

- *Awareness.* Is the brand well known in the marketplace?

- *Reputation.* Is the brand well regarded in the marketplace? Does it have high perceived quality?

- *Differentiation.* Does the brand have a point of differentiation? A personality?

- *Relevance.* Is the brand relevant for today's customers and today's applications?

- *Loyalty.* Are customers loyal to the brand?

BUSINESS STRENGTH

- *Sales.* Is this brand driving a significant business?

- *Share/market position.* Does this brand hold a dominant or leading position in the market?

- *Profit margin.* Is this brand a margin contributor? Or is the cost position or the market conditions such that margins are unfavorable?

- *Growth.* Are the growth prospects for the brand positive within its existing markets? Is the brand likely to gain share or participate in a growing market?

STRATEGIC FIT

- *Extendibility.* Does the brand have the potential to extend to other products either as a master brand or as an endorser?

- *Potential as platform for growth.* Is there an upcoming offering that could use this brand?

- *Business fit.* Does the brand drive a business that fits strategically with the direction of the firm? Does it support a product or market that is central to the future business strategy of the firm?

BRANDING OPTIONS

- *Transfer brand equity to another brand.* Could the brand equity be transferred to another brand in the portfolio by reducing the brand to a subbrand or by developing a descriptor?

- *Merge with other brands.* Could the brand be aggregated with other brands in the portfolio to form one brand?

- *Transfer equity to an umbrella brand.* Could the brand be sub-sumed under an umbrella brand (for example. as Word, PowerPoint, and Excel were placed under the Microsoft Office brand)?

Evaluate the Brands

Brands should be evaluated with respect to the criteria on the basis of the business and market knowledge of the CMO team and silo colleagues, supplemented by market research. A total score can provide a general measure of brand contribution; a low score across the criteria set would certainly suggest a review of the brand's role. Introducing weighting is an option; however, refining the analysis is usually not worthwhile given the subjectivity—it becomes overquantification. The evaluation should look to the future because it is future prospects that are at issue.

The profile of a brand across the criteria provides more detailed diagnostics. It can happen that a brand will have a place in the portfolio only if it meets some minimal level on one or two key criteria no matter how it does overall. For example, a low score on the strategic fit may be enough to signal that the brand's role must be assessed. Or if the brand is a significant cash drain then it might be a candidate for review even if it otherwise is apparently healthy.

Prioritize the Brands

The brands that are to live, be supported, and be actively managed should be prioritized or tiered in some way. The number of tiers will depend on the context, but the logic is to categorize brands so that precious brand-building budgets are allocated wisely.

The top tier will include the strategic power brands, those with existing or potential equity, that are supporting a significant business or have the potential to do so in the future. One type of second-tier brands would be those with a specialized role, such as a flanker brand. Another type would involve a smaller business, perhaps a niche or local business. The third tier would be brands with even less equity or business size and that would be candidates for consolidation.

Nestlé has long had in place brand portfolio prioritization. Twelve global brands are the tier-one brands on which the company focuses. Each of the global brands has a top executive who is designated as its brand champion. The executives in that role make sure that all activities enhance the brand. They have final approval over any brand extensions and major brand-building efforts. Nestlé has designated six of these brands— Nescafé for coffee, Nestea for tea, Buitoni for pasta and sauces, Maggi for bouillon cubes, Purina for pet food, and Nestlé for ice cream and candy— as the priority global brands within the company. Nestlé has also identified eighty-three regional brands that receive management attention from the Swiss headquarters. In addition, there are hundreds of local brands, which are considered either strategic—such as Dreyer's Grand Ice Cream, in which the headquarters is involved—or tactical, managed by local teams. Nestlé is not alone in prioritizing brands. P&G's turnaround since A. G. Lafley arrived was in part due to an ongoing effort to withdraw resources from or eliminate weaker brands so that the focus could be on the big brands.

A strategic brand can also be an umbrella brand in that it brings a set of existing brands under its umbrella, effectively reducing their status to descriptors. In 2003, Microsoft created a set of umbrella brands to group products providing similar value propositions to a similar primary target market that included Office, MSN, Xbox, Windows, and Microsoft

Business Solutions. Microsoft Business Solutions, for example, is an umbrella brand that represented a family of connected applications and services for small and midsize businesses. Included were Microsoft Business Solutions—CRM (a customer relationship management tool set), Microsoft Business Solutions—Analytics (reporting and budgeting), and Microsoft Business Solutions—Navision (business management solutions). Like the other umbrella brands, Microsoft Business Solutions enabled the company to reach this broad segment that none of the dozens of individual brands could.

One fruitful opportunity to achieve focus and clarity is to convert subbrands to a descriptive role or to replace them with descriptors. A descriptor brand will merit little or no resources and thus will no longer drain brand-building resources from other, more important brands. The use of descriptors makes sense when the subbrands have little brand equity, when a descriptor that works can be found, and when the master brand can play the driver role in the resulting product brand. Dell Computer in 1999 replaced a series of fifteen subbrands—that had little equity and were confused—with a series of descriptors. The brand E-Support became Dell Expert Services, Gigabuys became Dell Software & Peripherals, Ask Dudley became Dell Online Instant Answers, and DellNet became Dell Internet Access for Home.

There are other brand roles. One is the cash-cow role for brands that have equity and support a profitable business but should receive reduced resources. Still another is flanker roles for brands that are used to inhibit competitors from being too comfortable in a niche market. A premium brand might have a value flanker brand whose function is to prevent a competitor from getting a free ride in the value space to use as a growth platform.

The remaining brands should be eliminated, be placed on notice, or have their equity transferred to another brand.

- *Eliminate.* If a brand is judged to be ill suited for the portfolio because of performance, redundancy, or strategy fit issues, a plan to eliminate the brand from the portfolio is needed.

- *Place on notice.* A brand that is failing to meet its performance goals but has a plan to turn its prospects around might be put on an on-notice list. If the plan fails and prospects continue to look unfavorable, elimination should then be considered.

- *Transfer equity.* The customer loyalty to a brand to be eliminated can sometimes be retained by transferring the brand equity to another portfolio brand. Unilever transferred the equity of Rave hair products to Suave, and the Surf detergent products to All.

Develop the Revised Brand Portfolio Strategy

With brand priorities set, the brand portfolio strategy must be revised. Toward that end, several brand portfolio structures should be created. They could include a lean structure with a small number of master brands, perhaps only one, and a rich structure with more master brands involved and several levels of subbrands. There are probably several promising options in between. The idea is to create around two or three viable options with perhaps two or three suboptions under each.

The major brand portfolio structure options, together with suboptions, should be evaluated with respect to whether they:

- Support the business strategy going forward

- Provide suitable roles for the strong brands

- Leverage the strong brands

- Generate clarity both to customers and to the brand team

Implement the Strategy

The final step is to implement the portfolio strategy, which usually means a transition from the existing portfolio strategy to a target strategy. That transition can be made abruptly or gradually.

An abrupt transition can signal a change in the overall business and brand strategy; it becomes a one-time chance to provide visibility and credibility to a change affecting customers. So when Norwest Bank

The Centurion Case

A large manufacturing firm, here labeled as Centurion Industries, went through a strategic brand consolidation process when the CEO observed that its brand portfolio was too diffused and that future growth and market position depended on creating a simpler, more focused portfolio of powerful brands. The firm had grown in part by acquisition and now had nine product brands, three of which were endorsed by the corporate brand, Centurion, that served a variety of product markets that could be clustered into two logical groupings. Competitors with less brand fragmentation and more natural brand synergy had developed stronger brands and were enjoying share growth.

In the green business group, a brand assessment supported by customer research was conducted on its five brands. One, Larson, represented the largest business, had substantial credibility in that business, had high awareness levels, and could be stretched to cover the other four areas. It did have a visible quality problem, however, that was being addressed. The decision was made to migrate all the green business brands to Larson and to make the quality issue at Larson a corporate priority. The first migration stage was to endorse three of the brands with Larson and replace the fourth brand, which drove a small business, with the Larson brand. The second stage, to occur within two years, was to convert all the brands in the green business group to the Larson name and add an endorsement by the corporate brand.

acquired Wells Fargo and changed the name of Norwest to Wells Fargo, it had the opportunity to communicate new capabilities that would enhance the offering for customers. In particular, Norwest customers could be assured that the personal relationships they expected would not change, but they could also expect upgraded electronic banking services

In the blue business group, containing four brands, the brand Pacer emerged from the brand assessment stage as the strongest, especially in terms of awareness, image, and sales. Further, Pacer was in a business area closely related to that of the other three brands; thus using the Pacer brand for the blue business group was feasible. However, one of the four brands in the blue group, Cruiser, was an extremely strong niche brand with a dominant position in a relatively small market, and delivered significant self-expressive benefits to a hard-core customer base. Thus, it was decided that the Cruiser brand should be retained, but the balance of the blue group would operate under the Pacer brand. Both Pacer and Cruiser going forward would be endorsed by the corporate brand.

The end result was a brand portfolio involving three brands rather than nine, with all three consistently endorsed by the corporate brand. The critical decision was making the tough call that in the long run the brand portfolio would be stronger if niche brands were migrated to one of two broader brands. There were emotional, political, economic, and strategic arguments against each move. The fact that one exception was allowed made the case more difficult to make and to implement. Critical to organizational acceptance was the use of an objective assessment template, which clearly identified the dimensions of the decision and facilitated the evaluation. It helped that much of each assessment was quantified from hard sales and market research data. Also critical was the strategic vision of top management because at the end of the day, owners of some of the niche brands were not on board, and without a commitment from the top, it would not have happened.

because of the competence of Wells Fargo in that area. The name change reinforced the changed organization and the repositioning message.

An abrupt change in brands requires a positioning effort and substance behind the claims. The change in the brand promise must be communicated effectively and with credibility; otherwise, the one-time chance to make a statement will be wasted. And the business strategy must be in place to deliver on the brand promise, or the effort will backfire. If, for example, Norwest could not deliver the Wells Fargo technology, the best course would be to delay the name change until the company can deliver the substance behind the new position.

The other option is to migrate customers gradually from one brand to another. This is preferable when:

- No newsworthy repositioning will accompany the change.

- Customers who may not have high involvement in the product class may need time to learn about and understand the change.

- There is a risk of alienating existing customers by disrupting their brand relationship.

In the Centurion case (described above), the ultimate brand name, Larson, was first added as an endorser. Over time, the endorsement was to become more prominent and eventually become the master brand. Thus, customers gradually associated Larson with the product without disturbing the brand loyalty.

Prioritize Countries

Just as the prioritization of brands provides focus, so can the prioritization of countries provide focus to global marketing. The criteria for selecting priority countries should include:

- The future health of the market in the country, considering economic and competitive factors

- Marketing presence in terms of sales, market share, and ROI.

- Marketing strength as indicated by assets, such as brands, customer loyalty, and distribution.

- Growth potential both with existing and new products.

P&G prioritized counties, picking out ten countries out of the over 100 countries they are in to receive significant attention.[1]

Too Little Leverage—The Brand Extension Frameworks

A business strategy should leverage the key firm assets, such as the strategic brands. These brands often have high recognition, an aura of success, a customer following and, most important, strong associations and supporting marketing programs that can be the basis for entering new product categories or new countries. The CMO should consider every strategic brand as a potential growth platform. In addition, product or country expansion can enhance the brand asset by providing more visibility, a broader and deeper relationship with customers, stronger associations, and the credibility that comes from being good at more things in more places.

Dove provides a role model. In 1955, Unilever (then Lever Brothers) introduced the Dove "beauty bar." From 1955 to the early 1990s, Dove built a solid $220 million bar soap business. In a dozen years, it turned that into a $4 billion business by leveraging the moisturizer association and taking the brand into body washes, deodorants, facials (disposable face cloths), and shampoos, and expanding the market from a few countries to the whole globe. The Dove case shows the power of leveraging a brand, how one successful extension can provide the base for others, how cumulatively the brand can go from a product brand to a strategic brand platform, and how a powerful association supported by great products can work in country after country.

There are two distinct brand extension directions, and each has a framework that consists of a set of questions to consider: product expansion (taking the brand into new product categories); and country expansion (taking the brand into new countries).

Product Expansion

A host of brands besides Dove have expanded their business by entering new product arenas. Calvin Klein has leveraged fashion credibility from designer jeans to a host of items, including clothing of all types (such as underwear, jeans, and men's suits), fragrances, and eyewear. Braun leveraged its credibility in small personal care appliances to clocks and a wide range of household appliances, including food processors, hand blenders, coffeemakers, and curling irons. Disney, which started out with cartoon shorts, is now also strongly associated with feature-length film production, theme parks, clothing, toy stores, a hockey team, and cruise lines.

An overview of the product expansion decision is shown in figure 6-3. The key to successful product expansion is to identify or create a leverageable association; Dove, Calvin Klein, Braun, and Disney all did that well. Leverageable associations can come in many varieties, such as innovation (Apple has exciting products), quality (Lexus's relentless pursuit of perfection), product category credibility (Mercedes knows cars), product attribute/functional benefits (the taste of Hershey's), application credibility (Samsonite clothes for travelers), technological credibility (Honda and small motors), channel credibility (Avon and in-home selling), ingredient (Tylenol placed acetaminophen in a host of products, including sore throat, cold, sinus, and flu), user credibility (Gerber baby clothes), and brand personality/self-expressive benefits (Harley-Davidson clothing), and can be leveraged into new products.

To work, the associations must fit. There should be no discomfort with seeing the brand in the new context. A brand platform tends to be broader when the brand draws more heavily on associations that are not tied closely to a specific product. The wide scope of Virgin, for example, was

FIGURE 6-3

Leveraging the brand into new products

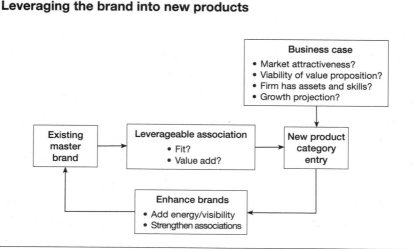

driven by a personality and style rather than a particular customer benefit that applies only to a single product category. The Amazon platform
is based on interacting with customers and a distribution method that can
be applied to a wide variety of products. In contrast, some brands are so
closely tied to a product that their potential to play a larger role is limited.

The associations should also be relevant and add value to the offering
in the new context. A good test is to ask respondents whether they
would buy the brand in the new context, and then ask why. If they cannot come up with a reason, there is a problem. Pillsbury popcorn did well
in concept tests but lacked a differentiating reason why people would
buy it. After initial success, it was blown away by the Orville Reden-
bacher's brand, which people did have a reason to buy. Many corporate
brands, such as Virgin, Sony, and Toyota, have successfully leveraged their
corporate brand. However, the challenge is to create relevance and differentiation in the new category. Relying on organizational associations such
as size, financial assets, and even innovation is risky if there are no differentiating associations that can be communicated in the new categories.

The focus in the product expansion decision is usually on what the
brand can do for the new offering. An equally important consideration
is what the offering will do to the brand. First, it should enhance the
brand by providing more visibility, energy, and customer exposure. Second, and more significant, it should enhance the brand by reinforcing
its associations or creating new associations that will move the brand toward its aspirational image and its role in supporting the future business
strategies of the firm. It is important to the brand health that the organization can deliver on the brand promise because failure to do so will reflect on the brand. There is brand risk involved.

A new product category also needs to be evaluated on the basis of
business criteria. First, how attractive is the new category in terms
of market size and growth, competitive intensity, and threats to its future
health? Second, is there room for a new value proposition? Will the entry
have been sufficiently differentiated? Dozens of studies have all shown
that a me-too product without a point of distinction usually fails. Third,
does the firm have the ability to succeed? Do it have the assets and skills
needed to deliver on the brand promise and be a strong competitor?

Fourth, will future products or line extensions provide a healthy growth trajectory?

In leveraging a strategic brand into new product areas, the sequencing of brand extensions becomes critical. What should be the order and timing of the new products that will ultimately be created? The idea is to gradually enlarge the brand scope and perhaps the brand associations as well. Ultimately, extensions that at one point would be an excessive stretch become feasible as the brand evolves into its new portfolio strategy. For example, Gillette meant razors when it introduced Gillette Foamy, a shaving product but not a razor. Gillette Foamy, closely linked to razors, was a bridge to the line of toiletries for men introduced under the Gillette series brand. The line supported the masculine side of Gillette, with very masculine packaging (a ribbed silver package). The Gillette series of toiletries would have been more of a stretch without the Gillette Foamy brand.

Strategic brands should have a long-term perspective with a vision of the ultimate scope of the brand and the route to get there. Leveraging a strategic brand should be very different from making one-off decisions to extend the brand into a different product arena. Such extension decisions tend to be ad hoc with a short-term perspective, resulting in suboptimal decisions with respect to a longer-term strategic view of the business, in part because considering future extensions may affect the associations that are created by the initial extensions.

Expanding the Global Footprint

Motivation to be global naturally leads to global initiatives to expand a firm's market footprint, a task that can be messy and difficult. Strategy development gets much harder when the context is a different language, an unfamiliar culture, new competitors and channels, and a very different set of market trends and forces. There are many routes to failure.

A key challenge is decide what country or countries to enter—and in what sequence. Entering any new market can be risky and take away resources that could be used to make strategic investments elsewhere. A frequently unforeseen consequence of global expansion is that healthy markets, especially the home market, are put at risk by this diversion of resources. It is thus important to select markets for which the likelihood of success will be high and the resource drain minimized.

Country or market selection starts with several basic dimensions that provide a country (or market) expansion framework:

- Is the market attractive in terms of size and growth? Are there favorable market trends? For many companies, China and India often appear attractive because of their sheer size and growth potential.

- How intense is the competition? Are other firms well entrenched with a loyal following, and are they committed to defending their position? Tesco, a major retailer in the United Kingdom, found that expansion into France was unattractive because of the established competition, whereas eastern European countries had much less formidable competition. As a result, Hungary was the first country in continental Europe that Tesco entered.[2]

- Are there political uncertainties that will add risk? In addition to the obvious risks of political instability, there are more subtle issues. Coca-Cola and PepsiCo were blindsided in India when a nongovernmental entity claimed to have found pesticide residue in their products. Despite their protestations and evidence that the claims were unfounded, their business took a 12 percent dive and their image suffered.

- Can the firm implement its business model in the country, or do operational or cultural barriers exist? How feasible is any adaptation that is required? Marks & Spencer, a UK retailer spanning food, clothing, and general merchandise, attempted to export its offerings and the look and feel of its stores to the Continent, only to find that those offerings had little appeal to Europeans.

- Can the firm add value to the new market? Will the products and business model provide a point of differentiation that represents a relevant customer benefit? Tesco has developed an Internet-based home delivery system for grocery retailers that adds value in many markets.[3] Nike, Pampers, and Heineken, for example, have been able to differentiate their brand the same way everywhere.

- Can a critical mass be achieved? It is usually fatal to enter countries lacking the sales potential needed to support the marketing and distribution effort needed for success.

A study of some 150 international expansion initiatives during a five-year period ending at 2000 showed that fewer than half avoided failure.[4] However, the examination of those that survived suggested that success was usually accompanied by four conditions. One of these reinforces the fact that a firm must be able to add value to the market by exporting the firm's value proposition. Another suggests that the firm must be able to achieve critical mass, although it is important to recognize that for some industries, such as computers or razors, the economics are based on global share rather than local share.

The other two conditions are instructive. Success is enhanced if the firm has:

- *A strong core.* A strong home market provides resources and experience that the firm can leverage in geographic expansion. It is a rare firm that finds success abroad without a successful home market that provides not only resources but an operations template.

- *A repeatable formula for expansion.* When the same model works in country after country, the risk of entry is reduced. Avon, for example, uses its direct model everywhere and has refined the execution to a science. If the business model has to be reinvented, the entering firm takes on an additional burden.

Wal-Mart's surprising failure in Germany illustrates that even a firm with a strong core business can struggle in a new market.[5] In 2006 Wal-Mart gave up a ten-year effort to have a successful presence in Germany.

It made several mistakes and misjudgments. The first CEO spoke only English and insisted that his managers do the same. The next CEO tried to manage from the United Kingdom. Much of Wal-Mart's value proposition was neutralized by conditions in Germany. The short shopping hours and the fact that Germans did not want assistance in the store, for example, undercut two of the features that helped make Wal-Mart successful elsewhere. Wal-Mart seemed to underestimate the major German competitors that did not provide much of an opening for a value offering. Finally, Wal-Mart failed to achieve the economics of scale needed to justify its infrastructure.

In addition to deciding which country to enter, firms need to decide how to sequence countries and how many countries to enter. A strategy of entering countries sequentially has several advantages. It reduces the initial commitment, allows improvement of the product and marketing program on the basis of experience in preceding countries, and provides for the gradual creation of a regional presence. Other factors, however, argue that global expansion should be done on as wide a front as possible. First, economies of scale, a key element of successful global strategies, will be more quickly realized and will be a more significant factor. Second, the ability of competitors to copy products and brand positions—a very real threat in most industries—will be inhibited because a first-mover advantage will occur in more markets.

The CMO Role

The CMO is usually in the best position to address the three issues—too many brands, too few priorities, and too little leverage. First, the CMO can take an organization-wide perspective, which is needed in addressing all three issues. Relative judgments are needed, since analyses that are restricted to silo markets will not be responsive to the problems. Second, the CMO team can provide an analytical, dispassionate analysis, thereby reducing the emotionality that is so much a part of these decisions. Third, the analyses require relatively sophisticated and nuanced judgments plus access to silo-spanning data and information. The CMO has the best chance to deliver on both. Finally, the assessments will need to look between silos and at combinations of silos, something that does not come naturally to silo executives.

For Discussion

1. What is the procedure, if any, to get approval to add a brand to the portfolio? Is it adequate, or should it be altered?

2. Does your firm have too many brands? What problems are they creating?

3. What are the key strategic brands in the firm? Do they receive an adequate share of the brand-building resources?

4. What brands have little equity and are receiving brand-building resources that could be better spent elsewhere?

5. What brands are candidates for product expansion? What are some product areas that should be considered?

6. What brands are candidates for country expansion? What countries or types of countries should be considered?

Chapter 7

Create Winning Marketing in a Silo World

*Good is the enemy of great. That is one of
the key reasons why we have so little
that becomes great.*

—Jim Collins, author, *From Good to Great*[1]

When there is no wind, row.

—Portuguese proverb

MARKETING PROGRAMS, especially in these days of media fragmentation, require implementation brilliance—"good enough" is not good enough. Organizations need brilliant, break-out-of-the-clutter marketing programs directed at priority markets. Great marketing not only is cost effective but will bring the silos together. A clearly outstanding idea or programs will turn resistance into support and enthusiasm.

The dilemma is how to rise above good to superior, if not brilliant, in silo markets while creating synergy and leveraging the scope of the organization. Complete silo autonomy potentially can lead to effective silo marketing but more often means that marketing is uneven and inefficient, and accesses a smaller pool of talent and resources. On the other hand, efforts to centralize marketing to create synergy often result in compromise, constraints, and an unmotivated silo team. The challenge is to make the silos assets instead of hindrances in creating brilliant cross-silo marketing.

The chapter addresses five questions:

- What are the routes to generating potentially great ideas that draw on the silo realities?

- How much scope and authority should the silo marketing team have?

- How many communication partners should you have?

- How do you allocate resources across silos?

- How do you sell the brand vision internally so that the marketing will become more consistent and reinforcing?

Creating Great Offerings and Marketing Programs in a Silo World

The existence of silos at once presents a challenge and an opportunity in creating marketing offerings and programs with impact. It is a challenge because the silos resist ideas that are "not invented here," and value and protect their autonomy. It is an opportunity because the silos represent a host of laboratories in which ideas can develop, flourish, and be refined.

There are two routes to effective offerings and marketing programs in a silo world: the silo route and central marketing route. Figure 7-1 illustrates. In the silo route, ideas originate in the silos, and the organizational challenge is to recognize brilliance, test the ideas, and leverage them into the other silos. In the central marketing route, a silo-spanning concept is created centrally and then applied, perhaps with adaptation, to the silos. Each can work, but each has challenges.

The Silo Route

The goal is to encourage silos to generate offerings or marketing programs and then leverage those that are successful. That means that the

FIGURE 7-1

Routes to marketing success in a silo world

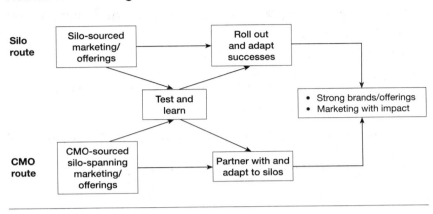

silos should have the bandwidth, motivation, freedom, capability, and tools to innovate. The culture and reward systems should be supportive, and there must be effective means to identify silo success stories and leverage them into other silos. The CMO team will make this more certain if it is involved in the management of the process.

The new offerings that silos create to win in their own markets may also work, perhaps with some adaptation, in other markets. McDonald's has gotten ideas from franchisees who are close to the market. In fact, one of the biggest product winners, the Egg McMuffin, was developed by a franchise manager who was initially motivated to create breakfast for himself. The Dove facial cleanser came from Japan and Taiwan. One key is to listen to the "fringe" markets and avoid a "not invented here" attitude. In a classic blunder, Xerox, in the 1970s, turned its back on a desktop copier because it was invented by Fuji-Xerox in Japan, only shortly thereafter to be blindsided by competitors with similar products.

Marketing programs developed in one silo can also often work in others. P&G finds exceptional ideas by empowering the country brand teams to develop breakthrough marketing programs. Once a winner is found, the organization tests it in other countries and rolls it out as fast as possible. P&G's Pantene Pro-V was a small brand, obtained with the purchase of Richardson Vicks in 1985, that had a modest but hard-core following. Efforts to expand the following in the United States and elsewhere were unsuccessful, but brand strategists struck gold in Taiwan when a positioning around the tagline "Hair so healthy it shines" was a winner. The concept and supporting advertising tested well in other markets and was subsequently rolled out to seventy countries, and Pantene is now one of P&G's twenty-three billion-dollar brands. McDonald's got the creative idea for its "I'm lovin' it" campaign form Germany. Coca-Cola's big winner, Zero, went to black cans because of the sales experience in Australia and the United Kingdom.

Sometimes, the silo with the largest market has the talent and resources to develop a winner and smaller markets can benefit from the innovation. That was the case with Nestlé's Dreyer's brand of ice cream. Dreyer's, a leading player in the world's largest ice cream market, the United States, created Dibs (bite-size chocolate-covered ice cream) and a slow-churned product that represented an advance in both taste and nutrition. Each were rolled out to other countries by Nestlé's central ice cream global marketing group.

The innovation need not come from within the organization. The silo units can be the dispersed eyes and ears of the organization across industries and across countries, identifying successes even from outside their industry that the organization could adapt to its needs. Learning comes from role models, firms that have hit home runs with new products or marketing programs. The Olympic skiing champion Jean-Claude Killy once said that "the best and fastest way to learn a sport is to watch and imitate a champion." That is true for marketing programs as well. It is not necessary to be the inventor; it is enough to recognize excellence and be able to adapt it.

The silo units must be equipped to come up with ideas in the first place. Creative thinking methods can help. One automobile brand, for example, used formal creative thinking exercises to develop a promotion in Turkey involving people searching for a "lost" car. The exercises included ideation without evaluation and generated several options. One option with the largest potential impact was selected for a second phase: how to make it feasible. The result was a home run.

The CMO Route

The CMO team can develop silo-spanning offerings and marketing programs that leverage the scale of the organization. Of course, a wide variety of marketing vehicles could drive silo-spanning marketing. Some could be service features, such as the Hilton HHonors loyalty program. Others could be Internet-based programs, such as Tide's Fabric Advisor or the Harley-Davidson Ride Planner, both of which span product silos. The challenge is to find ways to create executions that have an integrated flavor, break out of the clutter, resonate with the core target audience, and can be used over multiple product and country silos. Two of the most potentially powerful are brand visions and sponsorships.

A big idea can be a brand essence that provides inspiration and clarity of purpose to all the silos, including functional marketing silos. The best both capture and contribute to the business strategy and the culture and, by themselves, stimulate strategic initiatives. That describes HSBC as "the world's local bank," GE's "imagination at work," and the Lexus "Relentless Pursuit of Perfection." The Haas School of Business, as described earlier, developed a vision of "Leading Through Innovation" that provided direction and impetus for all the silos in the school, from the school curriculum to admissions, to placement, to executive education, to research centers, to the entrepreneurs center, and on and on. If everyone in the organization understands and believes, the brand promise has a good chance of happening. Later in this chapter, we will discuss communicating the brand internally, a key enabler to a great brand vision.

A major sponsorship is a program that can help get people to work together across silos. Samsung's remarkable brand elevation during a short time was in part due to its ongoing commitment to the Olympics, made in 1997, that will continue for decades. It helped put the company in the category of the top global brands in customers' minds. The sponsorship, of course, spanned all the company's silos. Its long-term commitment to the sponsorship allows the Olympic link to Samsung to grow over time and become part of the Samsung experience. When the CMO team finds an effective silo-spanning program, it should leverage

Coordinating Functional Silos—IMC

The challenge of integrated marketing communication (IMC) is that the functional silos, such as sponsorship, advertising, and digital marketing, are natural competitors rather than partners. The challenge of getting cooperation and consistency is formidable. How can excellence across silos emerge in this environment? Routes to excellence in the functional silo world are essentially the same as they are in the product and country silo worlds—either source programs in one of the functional silos and then give the other silos a supporting role, or have the CMO team develop a great idea and apply or adapt it to the silo space.

In the silo-sourced route, the marketing functional silos do their own thing as well as they can. When one gets a home run program, the others are realigned to support that program. The lead marketing program could come from any modality, such as a sponsorship, a promotion, a Web site, or an advertising theme. The key is the great idea that is instantly recognized as one that will get results in the marketplace. When that occurs, resistance melts. Everyone wants to be on the team driving a truly exceptional program, one that is so good that it does not require testing. Creatives from every discipline will simply nod their heads.

For example, in 2001 the BMW functional marketing silos were attempting to come up with a program in a cluttered automobile space. An observation by the digital team that it was possible to download a short film stimulated the creative people in advertising to embark on the BMW films program. Six top directors were asked to create with complete artistic freedom BMW commercials of six minutes or so, to be accessed on the Internet. The rest of the IMC team turned to support the effort. The budget was drastically reallocated, with much of it going to the production of the films. Advertising's role became one of driving people to the Web site. PR was directed toward getting buzz around the films. The whole effort was staggeringly successful in exposure of the films, the buzz about the programs, and car sales. The IMC point, however, is that the idea from one functional unit was so compelling that it created on-board acceptance by all the functional silos about their role in the program.

For Valvoline, NASCAR sponsorship connected to the sweet spot of its target audience. Most of the other communication efforts were directed at supporting the sponsorship, including promotion and advertising. In particular, the Valvoline Web site leveraged its racing sponsorship by providing racing information and inside stories about track experience to link to its core customers—those interested in NASCAR racing. Supporting the sponsorship greatly enhanced its connection to customers and its ultimate impact.

A second route to excellence is to generate a great idea in the CMO team and get the functional silos to support it. That is exactly what Hobart, the manufacturer of industrial kitchen appliances, did. Year after year, Hobart had told the world about the quality and newest features in its mixers or ranges, until one year it changed course. Instead of promoting products, it became expert in customer problems—hiring and training people, food safety, menus, and so on. All the functional silos were assigned supporting roles in implementing the idea. Well over a dozen white papers on the identified customer problems were prepared and attached to the company's Web site. The trade shows had an "ask the expert about your issues" component. Speeches and articles led the PR contribution. Even the advertisements were about customer issues. This activity involved a painful reduction in product promotion, but it advanced the cause of the Hobart brand and provided a link with customers that product promotion never could do. It also rather dramatically generated communication that was highly integrated.

the program into the silos, which should be encouraged and incented to develop supporting silo-based programs.

A sponsorship that is the cornerstone of the marketing program can be developed and owned by a firm as well; owning provides significant potential advantages. An owned sponsorship can be firmly linked to the sponsoring firm, and the associations and the cost can be controlled over time. Consider, for example, adidas's Streetball Challenge, a three-on-three basketball weekend tournament surrounded by a weekend party with music and games—very attuned to the core target segment. The sponsorship, which spanned both product and country silos, helped turn adidas around in Europe in the 1990s. Consider also the impact of the Avon Walk for Breast Cancer, which for decades has involved hundreds of thousands of women, has raised a meaningful amount of money for cancer research, and has provided substantial energy and good will for Avon and, of course, spanned the Avon silos.

Test and Learn

Ideas leading to offerings and marketing programs may be plentiful, but they must be tested not only to select or confirm success but to determine the reasons behind the success, and to learn how the ideas should be refined and adapted as they are introduced into different contexts. Having a multisilo organization provides a testing laboratory. A test-and-learn program consists of a set of experiments that, unlike ad hoc experimentation, should be ongoing, with experiments that build on each other. Unlike qualitative concept testing, test and learn will be real tests in real markets. If it is done well, a rapid rollout can result in preempting the offering or program in market after market.

Ideas must be screened before they are tested. A concept or program that is successful in one silo will not necessarily be so in others. In selecting which programs to export and to which silos, firms will find it useful to analyze the reasons behind the success. What is it about the silo and the target segment that helped enable success? What other silos will have similar characteristics? Such a thought process will avoid the waste of time and resources involved in rolling out programs that prove disappointing in other environments for reasons that could have been predicted. It will enhance the chance that the first few rollouts will be successful.

Centralizing global marketing, as Dell and others have learned, changes dramatically the test-and-learn program and market research in general. The test cells now have to be drawn from the global market, and choosing what countries to include in the test becomes an issue, with cost-benefit trade-offs to be made. Further, the task is often more strategic and demanding. Instead of fine-tuning marketing programs for one market, the new charge could be to find programs that will work in a much larger, more heterogeneous marketplace.

The Scope and Authority of the Silo Team

The role of the CMO team in designing and implementing or actively managing marketing programs will vary widely. It will depend, of course, on whether the dominant role or roles are as a facilitator, a consultant, a service provider, a strategic partner, or a strategic captain. But it is never that simple. The roles can vary over marketing activities, as was discussed in chapter 1. A CMO team that is primarily a facilitator may take on a strategic captain role for some activities, such as the visual presentation. On the other hand, in the strategic captain role, the CMO team will sometimes want the silo groups to adapt programs and be completely in charge of others that are inherently local.

Thus, the degree of control that the CMO team exerts will depend on the activity and the marketing program in addition to the team's dominant roles. Therefore, each marketing activity—such as logo use, packaging, positioning, advertising, sponsorships, Internet sites, and pricing, and marketing programs such as an environmentalist, or "green," initiative—can be categorized as to whether it is imperative, adaptable, or discretionary (see figure 7-2).

- Imperative activities and programs are those that the silo management must do—there is no room for modification. The CMO

FIGURE 7-2

Silo involvement and control in marketing activities

Imperative activities	Adaptable activities	Discretionary activities
Little silo control	Some silo control	Substantial silo control

team would manage the program and the budgets. The use of visual designs is often in this category.

- Adaptable activities and programs involve guidelines that are not rigid—they allow some room for local adaptation. Some budget flexibility will exist. Often, corporate advertising can be adapted to the silo context. Lord Horatio Nelson provides a role model. Before the Battle of Trafalgar, he discussed his strategy with his captains in great detail with the understanding that during the battle they were on their own tactically. It worked for Nelson.

- Discretionary activities and programs are those for which the local management has full discretion, including the budget. Local sponsorships may fall into this category.

For Shiseido, for example, the CMO team is responsible for domestic and international brand identities and positions, product development, and packaging. The output of its work in these areas generates global imperatives. The advertising is adapted to local markets, and the promotional activities are discretionary.

Making explicit the authority of the silo marketing team by activity and program so that there is no misunderstanding is important. Silo teams assuming more control than appropriate or failing to realize that they are expected to engage in discretionary activities or adapt programs to their context can result in lost opportunities or even disasters.

For any marketing activity or marketing program, the selection of the imperative, adaptable, or discretionary category depends on a series of questions:

- *Silo marketing talent.* Is the marketing talent available in the silo teams superior or even adequate? How capable is the local team at designing and implementing marketing programs? If the talent is weak, the authority should be less. A broader and more strategic issue is where should the functional expertise reside? Can redundancy be reduced and staff critical size be fostered by centralizing the talent around an activity? It is far better to have one group of people with a depth of competence in an area such as advertising or sponsorships who can support each other than many groups with shallow talent and capacity. When the silo sales base is small, the option of using silo-based functional teams often disappears. Automobile brands in small European countries must borrow from larger country efforts because they lack the sales base to develop their own.

- *Potential impact of the CMO's central marketing program.* Is the central marketing program worth imposing in silo units? Is it exceptionally effective with respect to its objectives? It can make sense to allow more adaptation until a home run central program is developed. Does the marketing program span markets and thus represent significant potential synergy and require cross-silo coordination? A major sponsorship such as the Olympics or the World Cup will need cross-silo cooperation and involvement to gain the needed scale economies—allowing silos to opt out may not be an option. Is the program central to building a strategic brand? If so, its success may merit priority over short-range silo objectives.

- *Uniqueness of the silo market.* How unique is the silo market in the context of the marketing program? If a global program, for example, is relatively culture free with universal appeal, then there is a reduced need to adapt it to the local country context. If, on the other hand, there are local sensitivities or customer motivations, then local knowledge and the freedom to adapt programs become necessary. Certainly, some GE programs might have to be adapted to make them work for GE Capital and GE Lighting, for example. A more extreme example is the use of nudes in Shiseido ads, which would be impossible in Arab countries.

- *Stress caused by withholding silo authority.* What alteration in budgets, reporting lines, and authority can be tolerated? What fights are worth winning? In the case of Visa, the integrity of the brand had the highest priority—the energy to fight battles was devoted to making sure that product offerings, such as charging for converting currency, were not generated that would compromise the brand promise.

In determining what should be in the imperative category, firms should recognize that there will always be an institutional bias toward the "we are different" belief. People like and understand their local markets and see little differences that others do not. Silos can easily defend the logic that a program imposed from outside will be suboptimal or even infeasible. And there is a "not invented here" syndrome, in which it is much easier to be enthusiastic about your own ideas and find a way to make them work than those of others, especially others with authority to force their ideas on you.

The most likely candidate for imperative status is often the visual presentation of the brand including its logo. There is usually little reason to have the logo and, more generally, the look and feel of the brand on packages, signage, letterheads, advertisements, and displays, which differ across silos. And there is an enormous upside to creating a common visual face. It will symbolize the common organization to customers and, perhaps more important, to employees, and it will cumulatively help build the brand.

In addition to visual presentation guidelines, other activities that can be centralized and result in imperative programs are marketing research methods, training, corporate PR, and corporate advertising. Major corporate sponsorship and product communication programs, however, are more contentious because they encroach meaningfully on budgets and control of basic functional tools.

While few programs will fall into the pure imperative mode, many will involve some level of adaptation. So if a global brand position and advertising campaign, such as P&G's Pantene campaign, is adopted, the country managers still can adapt the ad execution to their country. The adaptation may not be unconstrained—there might be some common touchstones that provide some direction. For example, all the Pantene ads use a model with great hair. Kao's Bioré, a skin care product, has a creative guideline to show skin in the visuals. Heineken makes it a point to show a social gathering of a few (not too many) people who are socially appealing and enjoying time together with Heineken. The hair, the skin visual, and the social setting help center the brand. But within those parameters, the silo groups still have some latitude.

The adaptation model also has the advantage of providing some ownership of the resulting brand-building product. One firm makes it a point to have NIH stand for "now improved here" instead of "not invented here," suggesting that the country team can raise a good idea to brilliance with clever local adaptation. The Henkel CEO has noted that local adaptation is both crucial and difficult—considerable talent and skill are required. For example, the concept that "a good detergent implies that you do not have to boil your clothes" works in some countries but does not translate directly into German—a local interpretation thus becomes necessary. Also "April freshness" has an association with spring in some countries but makes no sense in northern countries, where April is associated with the works of Richard Wagner.

Discretionary activities are those with few constraints. The silo team is free to innovate programs on its own with little oversight. Such programs will often be promotions or sponsorships that are local in nature. However, even in such cases, the brand identities should guide. In the case of Dell, the five tenets—direct model, simple, customized, value, and standards based—guide the country managers. The only universal imperative is the visual presentation and the proscription that all ads look and feel the same. The rest is basically discretionary.

Even when programs are discretionary, logic can get silo teams on board. The GE Money silo resisted the "imagination at work" theme at first but eventually came to believe that the corporate effort was so valuable, it was worthwhile to make it work for them. In the mid-1990s, a conglomerate of seventeen acquired financial companies with a corporate umbrella of Capital Holdings gave each the option of sticking with its name or changing it to the new corporate name, Providian. The few holdouts came around after seeing the support the company was giving to the new name. Sometimes it is good psychology to make an offer the silos cannot refuse rather than forcing them to do something.

Silo Managers' Authority Creep

A system should exist to ensure that the silo managers are operating within their authority. The best system will fail if it is not used or if it is misused. Making sure that it is working effectively is a key governance task. Thus, a set of reporting devices should allow the CMO team observer to know what parts of the system are being used, misused, or underused.

The CMO team can play a governance role by exerting authority or by having a channel of communication open to those with authority. Sign-off power makes the task easier. At Smirnoff, a Diageo brand, the CMO was at one time given the title of president of the Pierre Smirnoff Company, with veto power over local advertising campaigns. It is common for the CMO team to have sign-off authority over imperative programs such as the logos and visuals.

Even when authority exists, the CMO team should have a positive force and not be seen as autocratic, acting as the police who are seen as always telling silo managers what they cannot do. Otherwise, the prime task of creating a brand-building culture, where synergy and brilliance are fostered, will be compromised.

The process of getting silo mangers on the same page does not have to necessarily involve close supervision. In fact, it is far better if the brand is so clearly enunciated, the buy-in so strong, and the support of the culture and top management so visible that actions that are "on brand" are automatically taken. It is likely that strong culture firms such as Apple or Harley-Davidson have much less trouble with keeping the silo activities on brand than firms with weaker cultures and brand identities.

As the involvement and authority of the CMO team increase, governance issues usually decrease. Philips, a global maker of consumer electronics, lighting, and personal care products, brought in a CEO with a marketing background and an outsider as head of global brand management. The charge was to create a broad-based customercentric culture and a powerful global brand. Over the course of eighteen months, five regional brand champions were brought on who were empowered to allocate brand-building budgets. Supporting these brand champions were regional marketing councils drawn from marketing, PR, and sales positions across all business lines. A centralized consumer intelligence unit responsible for conducting consumer research and tracking and measuring the Philips brand across regions was created. The result was a CMO team with enhanced authority and respect.

Top management can play a direct role in governance by being involved in the brand. A major energy company has executive sponsors for segments of its information system. Nestlé has top executives playing a brand champion role for its major global brands. The Dell CEO takes a regular interest in the visual presentation of the brand. Sesame Workshop (SW), the nonprofit producer of the *Sesame Street* TV show, designated the CEO of SW International to be the brand champion of all international markets. The goal was to make sure that the *Sesame Street* program in all countries stays true to the brand when selecting partners in developing the shows, and in the final on-air proudct.

How Many Communication Partners?

Companies often use a host of agencies serving as communication partners. Dell once had nearly 750 agencies, when you include communication partners for advertising, packaging, promotion, trade shows, and so on. Another firm had over 1,100. IBM once had some 70 advertising agencies. Why? Why not consolidate?

The ultimate argument for silo-controlled agencies is that the key to creative strategy and execution is brilliance. The task is to identify the best people and the best organizations. Common sense dictates that brilliance will be dispersed throughout different organizations; no company or small set of companies will be able to deliver brilliance across product categories, countries, and functional areas such as advertising, design, and sponsorship. Restricting silos to using an affiliate of a global agency will deprive them of access to brilliance and in fact may doom them to using a mediocre agency not motivated by a fear of losing a client—the worst of all possible worlds.

A second and related factor, supported by research, is that brilliance is more likely to result from getting multiple ideas and selecting the best than from getting a single idea, no matter how good the authors are. The more varied the idea inputs, the better. Thus, having multiple agencies with different styles and backgrounds competing for the best idea is more likely to result in big ideas. Audi, for example, uses multiple ad agencies for that purpose. In Europe, five Audi ad agencies from different countries, termed the "Audi agency network," compete to be the lead ad agency creating the campaign. The losers are retained to implement the winning campaign in their countries. Because they are still involved with Audi, they are available for another round of creative competition in the future. The Audi approach reduces the cross-agency coordination problem while retaining the advantages of more talent working on the problem. Of course, it may be possible to use different offices from the same agency in a similar competition, but that approach will result in less intense competition and in creative styles that are less distinct.

Third, there is also an organizational argument for silo-controlled agencies. Silo units are better able to manage and direct the activities of communication partners simply because they are closer to the market and the market-driven strategy. Perhaps more important, silo control of agencies is symbolically and functionally important to the culture of autonomy and accountability that is the basis of the silo world. If the CMO team controls agency relationships, it will inevitably become an involved link affecting the perceived ability of the silo team to design and implement programs. Further, a change toward centralization is so threatening, so operationally different, and so potentially damaging to silo independence, that it will be stressful to the organization and place at risk the entrepreneurial spirit of the silo team.

However, the use of multiple agencies comes at a high cost in the modern media environment because of several associated problems. The most significant of these is the inconsistency of message across silos that not only creates a confused image but inhibits efforts to make the brand a strong, cohesive force in the marketplace and in the organization. Many firms have seen their brand morph into very different forms of look and feel and even different personalities, in part, because of the use of multiple communication companies, each with a lead strategy person. Even if the multi-agencies work well together initially, the spirit of competition usually prevails over that of cooperation over time.

A second problem of working with multi-agencies is economic inefficiency. Just the operations overhead of dealing with many account executives and research staffs—to say nothing of the multiple accounting departments—is wasteful. Further, there is rampant project overlap and task duplication throughout the process. This inefficiency is multiplied by the number of agencies, which, as noted, can exceed one thousand.

A third problem, often hidden, is that the organization does not leverage its size and scale. As a result, its presence in any one agency may not put it in the top-client category. Therefore, it does not get priority on the "A team." It is probably more important to get the best people in a firm rather than the best firm.

A fourth problem is a reduced ability of the CMO to influence or even control the communication programs of the organization. Having a central agency makes the task less challenging and time-consuming. Fidelity Investments, for example, centers the advertising task in a 260-person in-house group that provides a locus of brand power. This structure allows the CMO to manage more efficiency the different campaigns and their variants. Although the ads tend to be product focused, they are selected not by the product teams but by the agency that is primarily charged with improving the organization's advancement of the brand message about mutual funds, retirement programs, and investment advice.

A final problem is that multi-agencies make the challenge of creating integrated marketing communication (IMC) more difficult. As the discussion in chapter 3 noted, the trend is to form teams of agencies to provide coherent, consistent brand-building programs and the evidence suggests that such teams may have greater long-term success if they are drawn from one firm or at least involve affiliated firms. The logic is that the destructive internal competition would therefore be reduced.

A host of firms, frustrated with an inconsistent message across silos and being unwilling or unable to coordinate different agencies (that often pride themselves on being independent and having a strategic flair), have sharply reduced their agency list, particularly their set of ad agencies. One of the most visible and dramatic was IBM that, as previously noted, in the early 1990s reduced the ad agency list from well over seventy to one, Ogilvy & Mather. There have been many others. Dell, for example, reduced its ad agency list from six to one, and Samsung from five to one.

The use of a single ad agency does not preclude different expressions for different silos. Mercedes, for example, has a lead ad agency that creates a menu of five or so campaigns. The silos can then pick the one most suitable. If there are five basic brand strategies instead of fifty-five, and if the same brand vision and communication strategy drives all of them, campaigns can be developed with more focus.

Having the same ad agency does not at all automatically create a consistent message, even if all their offices share common processes and a common culture. A review of European advertising for McDonald's in the late 1990s, all done by the Leo Burnett agency, revealed that in some countries McDonald's was positioned as fashionable and exotic instead of wholesome.[2] In Norway, one ad showed the staff of a Chinese restaurant confronting customers with a "no hamburger" taunt while devouring a McDonald's hamburger in the kitchen. Ads in Spain showed a highly generic rush of smiling faces and upbeat music. Much of the advertising seemed themeless and oriented toward short-term sales rather than brand building.

To correct the problem, Leo Burnett convened a three-day meeting with the creative and account directors from six countries, supported by market research about food trends and customers and their motivations. The meeting goal was to agree on a core identity and brand essence that could drive the advertising in all six countries. Although the Norwegian participants were somewhat reluctant, a consensus emerged. McDonald's key associations were a wholesome family place, kids, speed of service, tasty food, and the McDonald's magic. The essence was that of a "trusted friend." Some negative associations to be neutralized were being "patronizing and smiling but not genuine."

The country shops then re-created advertising independently but driven by the same identity and essence. The result was advertising that reinforced McDonald's as providing a wholesome, family-oriented, safe place. But it still was very different from country to country. An ad from Sweden showed a working mother scheming to avoid a business meeting to take her daughter to McDonald's, only to find her boss there with his son. In Belgium, a boy, sensitive to the embarassment of new glasses, flirts with a girl at McDonald's and cheers up. In a British ad, a boy maneuvers his father into taking him to McDonald's, where the father runs into his estranged wife and, to the son's delight, chats with her. In Norway, a boy is led by a grandmother through a surrealistic city to McDonald's. But the inconsistencies were sharply reduced.

This vignette exposes some tough lessons. First, developing and imposing a brand identity for country managers is not easy, even when the local firms have the same name. It requires a compelling brand identity that works across countries, and strong, central guidance from people with adequate credibility and authority. Having a single communication firm can work, but do not assume that it will solve all the problems and relieve the strategist from oversight responsibilities. Second, some of this advertising is better than others. But individual agencies, even within the same firm, sometimes resist taking work from others, arguing that they are best able to create effective advertising in their country. How do you manage the trade-off between leveraging good ideas and local adaptation? How can more commonality be achieved without diminishing creative vitality? One key is leadership driven by the brand and a culture and system of local adaptation.

Allocating Marketing Resources Across Silos

Firms can often dramatically improve the effectiveness of marketing programs by allocating resources better. Two common problems result in poring money into areas that are suboptimal.

One problem is the "peanut butter" allocation model, where the marketing budget gets spread over too many silos, the result of each silo's creating its own marketing plan and budget. Instead, the allocation should be analytical, on the basis of two objectives:

- To focus on the strategic businesses and brands to make sure they are adequately funded. Silos with the largest sales and prior budgets inevitably get overfunded. Reallocating funds to the promising businesses and brands of the future or to markets such as China may pay future dividends, even though it may not be justified on the basis of near-term sales. L'Oréal has a "cow and calves" policy, whereby business managers are responsible for building businesses that will be the future as well as managing today's business.

- To reward those silo units that can demonstrate through experiments or market response that they have effective programs. Those that have no evidence that their marketing programs are linked to profitability or future strategic strength should not be so rewarded. That implies that the firm has accountability measurement models in play, perhaps involving a test-and-learn program and/or statistical analysis of time series data.

Another problem is the tendency to allocate resources toward products rather than building master brands, including the corporate brand. Too often the marketing budget tends to go to the product innovations of the day at the expense of building brands. Innovations sometimes create large organizational energy. The new "whatever" will seem exciting to the employees who are involved—even if it is neither newsworthy nor exciting to customers. Further, the success of the new product is often critical to the success of silos and their executives. As a result, new product offerings tend to drive marketing budgets. If the products are hot, such as the iPod or the Prius, that might be a successful strategy. However, too often the new offerings have a news value that is short-lived, are of interest to a narrow audience, and sometimes are marginally above boring. And product marketing can inhibit a cohesive brand focus along with a supporting consistent brand-building program. The risk is especially high for a corporate brand such as Bank of America or DuPont. And the plain fact is that at the end of the day people are buying HP, Toyota, Logitech, and IBM, and not the latest product improvements. Product-driven marketing is often overrated and underdelivers in the long-term.

Diverting resources from silo-based product-driven marketing toward building the silo-spanning brands (including the corporate brand) under the influence or control of the CMO often creates organizational tension. For silos to give up resources, especially for defensible areas of expenditure, is bound to generate pain and frustration. Making that happen requires a forceful committed CEO who is armed with a strategy vision and a persuasive narrative. But it can happen. As already noted, Lou Gerstner famously cut product marketing from 90 percent to 50 percent of the marketing budget early in his tenure at IBM. Hobart, the manufacturer of industrial kitchen appliances, described in the box, "Coordinating Functional Silos—IMC," earlier in the chapter, did something similar.

One key to making the product versus brand resource-allocation judgment is to evaluate exactly what is driving the purchase decision and use experience. Is it product refinements or the brand? The assumption that it is the product is often erroneous. Another key is to get the brand right, to have a cohesive brand vision that is capable of making a difference to customers. It is pointless to believe that just by moving money around, a master brand equity will automatically benefit. In fact, one study showed that how that budget is spent matters four times as much as the budget size.

There is an alternative between the budget's being controlled by the silo units and by the CMO. Several firms set aside part of the budget for the CMO to allocate to the silo teams. So the money ultimately goes to the silo units, but the CMO controls its allocation. The CMO can base the allocation on those silos that have programs that advance a master brand. That provides a way to encourage and sensitize managers to brand-building activities.

Communicating the Brand Internally

Having a strong brand, culture, and business strategy is the ultimate silo buster. A compelling vision will get all the silos sharing a brand to be on the same page. But employees will not automatically know about and believe in even the best vision. It takes a program to make that happen. An important challenge for the CMO team therefore, is to build the brand internally.

Building and enhancing a brand absolutely requires that employees and firm partners, such as agencies, know the brand identity, care about the brand, and are committed to protecting and enhancing it. The goal is to get employees and partners to:

- *"Hear it"*—to listen to the brand identity and position and understand it

- *"Believe it"*—to internalize it and to care about it

- *"Live it"*—to have it affect programs and behavior

There should be an expectation inside the organization that all activities and programs should be on brand. In fact, there is a school of thought, especially among service companies, that brand building could be justified if it were only an internal program, because if the brand is accepted internally, customers will inevitably get it as well.

The CMO can employ a variety of communication and learning tools. The key is to have an internal integrated communication program that will have splashes of news and excitement, will signal top management interest, will be effective, and will gain involvement and emotional commitment from the target audience.

At a base level, a brand handbook should put forth the brand identity. Effective ones will make sure the brand is shown from a variety of perspectives, verbally, visually, and with role models and metaphors. Unilever's most global brand, Lipton Hot Refreshment, has a detailed manual that is updated regularly and covers not only visual presentation but also an in-depth description of the brand from its associations to its personality. Thus, everyone in the firm worldwide has the answer to any brand integrity question at their fingertips. Sony has an Internet-based manual that allows employees, partners, and customers to see the Sony story, including its core belief ("We create technology that inspires people to dream and find joy"), to access the visual standards, to dialogue with Sony, and much more.

Videos can add music and action to the brand and can be especially useful to provide texture for new employees. Limited Brands, for example, has several retail brands, such as Limited, Bath & Body Works, Victoria's Secret, and Structures. For each, a brand video was created that showed images and music to nonverbally reflect the brand. It was used to help current and future employees understand the brand. Videos are particularly good across cultures because visual imagery and music are a universal language.

A handbook and a video by themselves are passive teaching devices. The challenge is to motivate people to use them. It helps if they are readily accessible, if they are easy to use, and if their use is accepted and commonplace. One key is to train people throughout the organization who can be resources for others. Another is to make sure that the guidelines are followed and to identify those business units that depart from them.

A personal connection with the brand group can be helpful especially if the interaction involves a dialogue rather than lecture presentations. Dolby sound systems instituted a global brand manager position in 2001 to develop a brand strategy and brand portfolio strategy across products and countries and to develop a more dynamic visual design. The prime vehicle for brand assimilation during the first year was the global brand manager's making presentations and holding workshops for the various firm operating units. So the country managers got to learn and, more important, discuss the brand direction in a personal, interactive forum.

Communicating the brand is a lot easier if the CEO links it with corporate strategy and culture and talks brand. Certainly, that has been the reason that the brand developed clarity at Sony, Apple, Patagonia, MUJI, and elsewhere where the CEO has been directly involved. If the fundamental culture and priorities are linked, employees are more likely to "hear it, believe it, and live it." This task gets the CMO and the team into organizational culture building and change with all the associated tools.

A challenge is to move beyond a passive communication program to one that will engage employees. One route is to have a contest to select a name, a tagline, or examples of living the brand. Mobil (now Exxon-Mobil), for example, asked its employees to nominate programs or actions that best reflected the core identity elements of the Mobil brand: leadership, partnership, and trust. The winners were honored guests at a major car race of which Mobil was one of the sponsors. There were over three hundred entrants plus undoubtedly thousands who gave it some thought and discussed the contest entrants. The result was not only involvement and excitement but also some vivid role models for the brand.

Involving the employees in brand building can work. Ideas can be sought for brand-building programs that could include PR articles or special events. Simply informing employees about what is being done is worthwhile. BMW's policy of showing advertisements to employees before showing them to the general public has proved to be very effective in gaining employee buy-in and enthusiasm for the brand.

The introduction of a new brand identity or position provides an opportunity to communicate internally with some sense of news and excitement. Nissan, with a new CEO and a strong emphasis on developing the Nissan brand, stimulated a major brand effort to energize the Nissan family behind the brand and its new direction. The launch of the effort started with a celebratory event hosted by the president and senior executives to generate excitement and demonstrate commitment for the new brand initiative. The new consumer brand campaign added energy and direction. A brand education "action pack" included a videotaped message from the CEO and others and a PowerPoint presentation. Honda introduced its brand strategy and guidelines with a president's message and video.

There should be a close working relationship with the HR group, which typically has control of the internally focused culture and values of the firm, including training and culture-building activities, to make them come to life within the organization. The CMO team will often be charged with creating an externally focused brand identity and assimilating that through the organization. Most organizations will experience overload and confusion with two such efforts. The goal should be to reconcile the culture and values with the brand identity. Ideally, the brand vision should be a major subset of the values statement. If so, they can reinforce and support rather than confuse and detract. To achieve that goal, there should be an explicit effort to coordinate at the time the brand identity is created and when the brand assimilation program is designed so that the relationship to firm culture and values is clear.

When the brand reflects a compelling business strategy, is consistent, reinforces the culture and values of the organization, and achieves buy-in by the employees and partners, the silo issues will recede or be easier to address.

For Discussion

1. What are the most effective marketing programs of your organization and its competitors in the last five years? Did the ideas come from silos or the CMO team? What is the mechanism to distribute the best ideas of the silos? Is it working?

2. Put all the visual representations of the major strategic brands on a wall. Are they consistent and do they reinforce the brand message? If not, why not?

3. For what activities do the silo teams have discretionary authority? Authority to adapt? Is that working?

4. How many communication partners of all types are there? Is the number optimal?

5. How are the marketing resources allocated across silos? What silos are underfunded?

6. Evaluate the internal brand-building program.

Conclusion

The CMO's First Ninety Days

Self-conceit may lead to self-destruction.

—Aesop, "The Frog and the Ox"

Don't manage, lead.

—Jack Welch, former CEO of GE

W HAT SHOULD A CMO do during the first ninety days of a new or revitalized job? What should be the first-year agenda? The importance of getting off to a good start and avoiding a bad one is crucial for anyone undertaking a change agent role, even if the change has an extended time horizon. The danger is to get wrapped up in the day-to-day operations and fire-fighting meetings.

The early efforts should have two prongs. The first should be an assessment of the organization's capability to span silos, to generate cross-silo communication, cooperation, synergistic programs, and resource allocation in the face of silo barriers. The second be an action plan—what activities and actions and, most of all, with what priorities?

Assessing the Organization's Capability to Span Silos

Figure C-1 is an assessment guide that provides a road map for a comprehensive audit of the silo world. Each of the fourteen dimensions can be evaluated on a ten-point scale with respect to the organization's capability and performance with a rating of 10 meaning *exemplary*. The first eight of these dimensions represent enablers of silo-scanning marketing. The next six represent the presence or absence of cross-silo successes.

A total score can suggest a global judgment about the organization, whether silo spanning is a competitive advantage or liability. The assessment on the individual dimensions should indicate where the areas of weakness and opportunity lie. Where is the organization being held back? If there is broad weakness it will usually be useful to prioritize the eight enablers. If only a few of these are not in place, it will be difficult to avoid having the silo structure inhibit potential performance. The first dimension, the CMO team, is of special interest because its performance will be the driver of CMO programs and will be critical to achieving CMO goals.

Each dimension has several associated questions that serve to provide texture and perspectives to the analysis. Other questions might be added. Addressing the questions should provide depth of understanding of the organization's capability. They should also provide some diagnostic information as to exactly why the organization is weak on that dimension and what direction remedial efforts should take.

The assessment exercise, especially the work on the last six dimensions, should lead to a rationale for change. What exactly are the problems or lost opportunities that require the organization to make changes and the CMO office to get more resources and authority? These problems and lost opportunities should be as vivid and motivating as possible, illustrated with specific anecdotes. They should show that a potential competitive edge is being lost or that a competitive disadvantage is being created.

A key to getting a complete, honest picture is to sample people from a variety of silo contexts making sure that people of different level and

FIGURE C-1

Capability of spanning silos—audit

ORGANIZATIONAL ENABLERS OF SILO-SPANNING MARKETING

The CMO team

- Does the CMO team have defined roles? The right product and country scope?
- Is it sought after, accepted, tolerated, or avoided by the silo groups?
- Is the CMO team effective? Does it add value?
- Is the team moving in the right direction with the right speed toward resolving silo issues?
- Does the CMO have the right balance of authority and budget control by marketing activity?
- Does the CMO team create or have access to customer and marketing knowledge?
- Does the CMO team interact with the silo marketing groups effectively?
- Does the CMO team support centers of excellence focusing on topics or functional areas that span silos?

CEO support

- Is the CMO given adequate authority and resources?
- Does the CEO support the CMO and the need to reduce silo barriers?
- Does the CMO have a seat at the executive strategy table?

Cross-silo communication

- Are events and meetings effective at creating contacts and relationships that are used?
- Do people reach out to others outside their silo?
- Are silo personnel networked? Is networking encouraged?
- Is there a managed system of information networks that is healthy and effective?

The intranet-based information system

- Is there an intranet-based knowledge hub that is user friendly?
- Does the knowledge hub contain relevant and easily accessed information?
- Is it used extensively and appropriately?

The use of teams

- Are cross-silo teams assigned to handle the major cross-silo issues?
- Are the active cross-silo teams effective?
- Are there programs to measure and improve team performance?
- Are there enough active teams or is there a need for more?

The marketing planning system

- Is there a marketing planning system that is used by all the silos?
- Does it have common templates and frameworks?
- Does it drive strategy or is it considered a formality to get through?

Measurement and research

- Is there a common tracking data stream across silos?
- Is brand equity adequately measured?
- Is there a test and learn system? Is it ad hoc or ongoing? Does it include country silos?
- Is there a market research capability residing within the CMO team?

Marketing capabilities

- Are the functional marketing capabilities a strength or weakness overall?
- Are there redundancies and the lack of critical size in the functional marketing staffs?
- Is the talent level adequate? Are hiring and training programs in place to remedy any talent gaps?

(continued)

FIGURE C-1 (*continued*)

Capability of spanning silos—audit

SILO-SPANNING MARKETING SUCCESSES/FAILURES

Resource allocation

- Are marketing resources allocated over product, country, and functional silos optimally?
- Are there models and processes in place to objectively allocate marketing resources over silos?
- Are the major strategic brands prioritized? Are they supported adequately?

Managing silo-spanning brands

- Do brands that span silos have positions and messages that are inconsistent and undercut the brand equity in important markets?
- Is there a mechanism to adapt the brand to different contexts without creating inconsistency?
- Should some brands be moving toward having a standardized brand and marketing program?
- Are there healthy internal brand programs?
- Are there aggressive programs to leverage a strong brand into new products or countries?

Organization-wide brand portfolio strategy

- Are there too many brands with resources spread too thin?
- Is there an objective organization-wide approach to approve new brands to prevent brand proliferation?
- Are the organization-wide strategic brands identified and given adequate resources?

Silo-spanning marketing programs

- Are there effective marketing programs that span silos? Should there be more?
- Are there processes to create or propose them?
- Is the implementation of cross-silo programs smooth and successful? Does stress build over time?
- Are there too many communication partners? Is there a coordination problem?

Leveraging silo success

- Are there silo marketing successes that have been effectively exported to other countries or markets?
- How effective is the system to test and learn potential marketing successes?
- How effective is the ability of the firm to roll out successes?

Silo-spanning offerings

- Is there an understanding of customers and markets that spans silos?
- Do cross-silo offerings get proposed?
- Are go-to-market strategies of cross-silo offerings effective? Are there long-term success stories?

function positions are included—the elephant can look different from different perspectives. In addition, it is helpful to talk to people outside the organization, to customers and communication partners. Too often problems exist that were not apparent to insiders. Lou Gerstner, when he took over IBM, inaugurated Operation Bear Hug, in which each of the top fifty executives and their direct reports were to visit a minimum of five large customers during a three month period and write a report on each.[1] The message was that customers were frustrated by IBM's silo orientation, which generated redundant sales calls and relationships and inhibited desired systems solutions. The customer voice made the problem convincing and dramatic.

Benchmark role models are useful to gain perspective. Within the organization, identify silos that seem to reach out and others that are isolated. Study both for insights into what works and what doesn't and what should be the attainable short-run and long-run standard. The existence of silo-spanning success stories inside the organization makes it tough to argue that it can't work here. The more specific and detailed they are, the better.

Benchmarks should also be sought outside the organization, even outside the industry. There can be a tendency to generate a low bar because what was done before seems adequate. A dramatic role model outside the organization can provide both an aspirational target showing what is possible and also a road map for how to get there.

Action Plan—Prioritizing Short- and Long-Term Goals

The challenge is to determine what should be the immediate priorities in terms of time, resources, and personal credibility. What should be accomplished in the near term, six to twelve months? Then what are the long-term objectives? What can and should be accomplished in the three- to five-year framework?

The CMO should base both sets of priorities in part on two dimensions. First, what is the impact of the activity if it is accomplished? Will it remove a barrier or an inhibiting force? Second, what is the difficultly of accomplishing the objective? Is it feasible? There is a trade-off. A modest doable goal may stimulate a worthwhile short-term activity.

Figure C-2 provides a suggested list of fifty-one priority programs organized into fourteen dimensions that correspond to the fourteen dimensions of Figure C-1. The CMO could evaluate each of the potential programs in terms of its impact and its feasibility using a pair of ten-

FIGURE C-2

Priority objectives and activities

	Impact	Feasibility	Long-term or short-term priority

ORGANIZATIONAL ENABLERS

The CMO team
- Clarify the roles of the CMO team by activity
- Gain acceptance of the CMO team
- Move up to a strategic partner or strategic captain role for certain activities
- Determine what should be the province of the silo teams in the short-term and long-term by marketing activity
- Review the product or country scope of the CMO office
- Explore organizational forms:
  o Create liaison, integrator roles
  o Create matrix structure
  o Disperse the marketing team
- Create centers of excellence focuses on topics or functional areas that span silos
- Develop a program to create or get CMO team access to customer knowledge

CEO support
- Get the CEO to think that marketing is strategic and key to the priorities of the business strategy
- Get the CEO involved
- Obtain the necessary authority and resources to fulfill the job expectation
- Gain a seat at the executive strategy table

Cross-silo communication
- Plan events or meetings that will create cross-silo relation-ships and communication's are used
- Create networks of people around topics of interest together with an organizing team and a supporting intranet site
- Create a culture of cross-silo communication

The intranet-based information system
- Create or upgrade the intranet knowledge hub, making it more effective
- Improve participation in the intranet knowledge hub

The use of teams
- Create teams to tackle the biggest problem areas
- Upgrade the operations of existing teams

The marketing planning system
- Improve the marketing planning system
- Get the silos to use the same marketing planning system
- Develop a process for each silo to create a brand identity or vision that will drive marketing

(continued)

FIGURE C-2 *(continued)*

Priority objectives and activities

	Impact	Feasibility	Long-term or short-term priority

Measurement and research

- Develop research methods that will yield cross-silo insights and performance indicators
- Develop measures of silo performance and brand equity
- Institute a tracking database
- Develop a test-and-learn capability that represents an ongoing refinement of offerings

Functional marketing capabilities

- Upgrade the talent of the central marketing group
- Upgrade the silo marketing talent
- Centralize some functional teams

SILO-SPANNING MARKETING

Resource allocation

- Develop analytical methods and frameworks to evaluate silo businesses
- Identify the strategic brands and businesses
- Allocate the marketing resources across silos

Managing silo-spanning brands

- Get the brand identity and position right; make sure it is enunciated clearly
- Measure the consistency of message and make adjustments
- Develop a program to adapt brands to silo contexts
- Create a brand building program
- Develop an internal branding program
- Consider the product or country expansion of the major master brands

Organization-wide brand portfolio

- Initiate a brand priority assessment process

Managing silo-spanning marketing programs

- Identify early wins—programs that will have little resistance, can be done in a reasonable time frame, and that are visible
- Tighten the visual presentation of the master brand
- Identify priority marketing programs
- Create some home-run marketing programs that break out of the clutter
- Develop expertise in programs areas that have the potential to span silos such as sponsorships and Web site–based programs
- Determine and implement policy regarding which marketing activities should be viewed by the silos as discretionary and what should be adaptable
- Create a program to improve the management of cross-silo marketing programs
- Reduce the number of communication partners

(continued)

FIGURE C-2 *(continued)*

Priority objectives and activities

	Impact	Feasibility	Long-term or short-term priority
Leveraging silo success			
• Develop a process and culture that allows silo-based exceptional marketing programs to emerge			
• Identify a process to recognize those programs and test and roll them out expeditiously			
Silo-spanning offerings			
• Develop a process based on an understanding of markets and customers for cross-silo offerings to emerge			
• Develop a competence in managing silo-spanning offerings			

point scales. These evaluations should help determine if the program should represent either a short-term priority or a long-term priority. The output should be a clear set of both short-term and long-term programs to implement, with priorities established for each.

In setting priorities, the CMO should basically divide the activities and associated roles into several groups. First are those that the central marketing group is now doing. Is the performance weak, adequate, or outstanding? What resources or changes need to be made to improve the performance, to make it outstanding? Second, what activities can be taken on without stressing the organization? Will these be worthwhile given the resources available? Third, of those potential activities that involve stressing the organization, which will make the most significant impact on strategy? What resources and programs will be needed to make progress?

A key issue is the time frame. Ambitious timetables are sometimes needed and possible when there is a crisis and the CEO is leading the charge, as was the case for IBM in the early 1990s and McDonald's in the early 2000s. However, in the absence of crises, being an aggressive change agent may be risky, may result in a short tenure for a CMO, and, worse, may set back the ability of the firm to address silo issues. Visa, for example, developed a common updated visual presentation, a revised global brand architecture, and the use of a single media firm—big achievements in its environment. But it took five years and represented a small part of the potential progress that still remains. Chevron centralized much of the silo marketing staff, first in Asia in a two-year effort and then for the whole firm, involving another three or four years. CMOs who inappropriately take on a change agent role with a short time horizon given the goals risk a damaging flameout.

Objectives and priorities are not enough, of course. Ultimately, the CMO needs programs to achieve objectives. Program success often goes beyond operational competence to influencing organizational culture, structure, processes, and people. It is a tough job that involves political astuteness, persuasion, and inspiration, but a job that can sometimes mean the difference between success and survival.

Keep Your Eye on the Ball—Focus on Silo Problems

As noted at the outset of the book, the all-too-common instinct of forcing centralization and standardization on the organization can be dysfunctional, even resulting in a flameout of the CMO team. Reducing silo authority, making the organization more centralized, and moving toward more standardized offerings and marketing programs is often needed and appropriate. There is, without question, a marked trend in that direction. However, these changes should not be goals in themselves but rather routes toward reducing the silo-driven problems (namely those represented in the fourteen dimensions of the capability audit). Such changes can be summarized in the six objectives of the CMO team introduced in the introductory chapter:

- Improve allocation of marketing resources.
- Foster more coherent and linked brand strategies.
- Develop silo spanning offerings and programs.
- Improve marketing management competence.
- Leverage silo successes.
- Foster communication and cooperation.

There are moments in the history of an organization when it is feasible and necessary to create or adjust a CMO office so that it plays a strategic partner or strategy captain role. That can be the best or even the only way to make changes that could be crucial to the health or even survival of a business strategy. However, it should also be clear that assuming the nonthreatening roles of facilitator, consultant, or service provider can lead to significant changes without stressing the organization, especially if the CEO can be made an involved supporter of the effort. The result can be an organization that retains much of the decentralized structure that has served it well but with silo units that work as team members. And progress should be visible toward the ultimate goal of creating stronger offerings and brands and effective, synergistic, effective marketing strategies and programs.

For Discussion

1. Assess the silo organization using the audit dimensions shown in figure C-1. Identify areas of strength and weaknesses.

2. What is the action plan for the first months and year? What are the priorities? What are the long-term, three- to five-year priorities and objectives?

Notes

Introduction

1. "What Would You Like to See Go Away in 2008?" *Brandweek*, December 17, 2007, 26.

2. Karl Greenburg, "ANA Survey Finds Most Struggle with Parochial Structures," *Marketing Daily*, May 30, 2008.

3. Siebel Web site (http://www.oracle.com/siebel).

4. Greg Welch, "CMO Tenure: Slowing Down the Revolving Door" (blue paper, Spencer Stuart, 2004).

5. Tom Agan, an insightful colleague and brand strategist, participated in many of the early interviews.

Chapter 1

1. Greg Welch, "CMO Tenure: Slowing Down the Revolving Door" (blue paper, Spencer Stuart, 2004), 4.

2. An elaboration of the IBM story can be found in Louis V. Gerstner Jr., *Who Says Elephants Can't Dance?* (New York: HarperBusiness, 2002), chapters 6, 7, and 8.

3. Angel Alloza, Director of Reputation, BBVA, interview with author, October 10, 2007.

Chapter 2

1. "Marketers Make Their Case," *Advertising Age,* July 9, 2007, 29.

2. *Are CMOs Irrelevant?: Organization, Value, Accountability, and the New Marketing Agenda,* Association of National Advertisers/Booz Allen Hamilton, November 2004.

3. Rajat Gupta and Jim Wendler, "Leading Change: An Interview with the CEO of P&G," *McKinsey Quarterly*, July 2005.

4. Jim Collins, *Good to Great: Why Some Companies Make the Leap—And Others Don't* (New York: HarperBusiness, 2001), 164–166.

5. Ellen Lewis, "Case Study: Unilever, the Marketing Academy," *Brand Strategy*, January 5, 2004.

Chapter 3

1. Alfred D. Chandler Jr., *Strategy and Structure: Chapters in the History of the Industrial Enterprise* (Cambridge, MA: MIT Press, 1969).

2. Alfred P. Sloan Jr., *My Years with General Motors* (New York: Doubleday, 1964), chapter 6.

3. David Court, Thomas D. French, and Trond Riiber Knudsen, "A Conversation with Four Senior Marketers," *McKinsey Quarterly*, no. 2 (2005): 26.

4. Nancy Giges, "McCann World Group at 10," *Advertising Age*, October 22, 2007.

5. Jon R. Katzenbach and Douglas K. Smith, "The Discipline of Teams," *Harvard Business Review*, March–April 1993, 112.

6. Ibid., 113.

7. Tom Kelley and Jonathan Littman, *The Ten Faces of Innovation* (New York: Doubleday, 2005), 2.

8. A good overview of cultural differences appears in Deborah L. Duarte and Nancy Tennant Snyder, *Mastering Virtual Teams: Strategies, Tools, and Techniques That Succeed* (San Francisco: Jossey-Bass, 2006), 56–66.

9. Geert Hofstede, *Culture's Consequences: International Differences in Work-Related Values* (Thousand Oaks, CA: Sage Publications, 1980).

10. Justin Sheck and Bobby White, "'Telepresence' is taking hold," *Wall Street Journal*, May 6, 2008.

11. Arvind Malhotra, Ann Majchrzak, and Benson Rosen, "Leading Virtual Teams," *Academy of Management Perspective*, February 2007, 60–70.

Chapter 4

1. For an elaboration of this business strategy framework, see David A. Aaker, *Strategic Market Management*, 8th ed. (Hoboken, NJ: Wiley, 2008), chapter 1.

2. For a summary, see David A. Aaker and Erich Joachimsthaler, *Brand Leadership* (New York: Free Press, 2000), chapters 2 and 3.

3. Jan Gerzema and Edward Lebar, *The Brand Bubble* (San Francisco: Jossey-Bass, 2008).

4. Jennifer Aaker, "Dimensions of Brand Personality," *Journal of Marketing Research* 35 (August 1997): 347–357.

5. Jennifer Aaker, Veronica Benet-Martinez, and Jordi Garolera, "Consumption Symbols as Carriers of Culture: A Study of Japanese and Spanish Brand Personality Constructs," *Journal of Personality and Social Psychology* 81 (2001): 492–508.

6. Emi Osono, Norihiko Shimizu, and Hirotaka Takeuchi, *Extreme Toyota: Radical Contradictions That Drive Success at the World's Best Manufacturer* (Hoboken, NJ: John Wiley & Sons, 2008), chapter 7.

7. Prema Nakia, "Is Global Branding Right for You?" http://www.i-b-t.net/.

8. "A Seat at the Table," *Hub*, September–October 2004, 2.

Chapter 5

1. Theodore Levitt, "The Globalization of Markets," *Harvard Business Review*, May–June 1983, 92.

2. Thomas L. Friedman, *The World Is Flat* (New York: Farrar, Strauss, and Giroux, 2005), 176–191.

3. Jean-Noel Kapferer, "Is There Really NO Hope for Local Brands?" in *Global Branding*, ed. Pedro Sousa (Boston: Marketing Science Institute, 2000), 5–7.

4. "Heading for the Exit," *Economist*, August 5, 2006.

5. Erin White and Jeffrey A. Trachtenberg, "One Size Doesn't Fit All," *Wall Street Journal*, October 1, 2003.

6. David A. Aaker and Bob Jacobson, "The Strategic Role of Product Quality," *Journal of Marketing* (October 1987): 31–44; and David A. Aaker and Bob Jacobson, "The Financial Information Content of Perceived Quality," *Journal of Marketing Research* (May 1994): 191–201.

7. "Esso—Should the Tiger Change Its Stripes?" *Reputation Impact*, October 2002, 16.

8. Douglas B. Holt, John A. Quelch, and Earl L. Taylor, "How Global Brands Compete," *Harvard Business Review*, September 2004, 68–75.

Chapter 6

1. Rajat Gupta and Jim Wendler, "Leading Change: An Interview with the CEO of P&G," *McKinsey Quarterly*, October 15, 2007, 3.

2. Victoria Griffith, "Welcome to Tesco, Your Local Superstore," *Strategy+Business*, First Quarter, 2002, 95.

3. Ibid., 94.

4. James Root and Josef Ming, "Keys to Foreign Growth: Four Requisites for Expanding Across Borders," *Strategy & Leadership* 34, no. 3 (2006): 59–61.

5. "Heading for the Exit," *Economist*, August 5, 2006.

Chapter 7

1. Jim Collins, *Good to Great: Why Some Companies Make the Leap . . . and Others Don't* (New York: HarperBusiness, 2001), 1.

2. This story is drawn from John Heilemann, "All Europeans Are Not Alike," *New Yorker*, April 28 and May 5, 1997, 176–179.

Conclusion

1. Louis V. Gerstner, Jr., *Who Says Elephants Can't Dance?* (New York: Harper Books, 2002), 50.

Index

About the Author

DAVID A. AAKER is the Vice Chairman of Prophet, a brand-driven strategy consulting firm; Professor Emeritus of Marketing Strategy at the Haas School of Business, University of California, Berkeley; and an adviser to Dentsu Inc. A recognized authority on brand and business strategy, he is the recipient of MIT Buck Weaver Award for contributions to the advancement of theory and practice in marketing science and was named as one of the top five most important marketing/business gurus by a survey of marketing executives. The author of over one hundred articles, Aaker has won awards for the best article in the *California Management Review* and (twice) in the *Journal of Marketing*. His fourteen books, which include *Strategic Market Management* (8th edition), *Managing Brand Equity*, *Building Strong Brands*, *Brand Leadership* (coauthored with Erich Joachimsthaler), and *Brand Portfolio Strategy*, have been translated into eighteen languages and have sold around one million copies. One of the most quoted authors in marketing, he is an active consultant and speaker throughout the world. Aaker is on the Board of Directors of California Casualty Insurance Company and the Food Bank of Contra Costa and Solano Counties.